jane grosslight

illustrations by jeffery w. verheyen

LIGHTING

KITCHENS AND BATHS

DURWOOD PUBLISHERS
BOX 37474 TALLAHASSEE, FL 32315

Published by Durwood Publishers
Printed in the United States of America

This book and its companion Work Booklet, ISBN 0-927412-03-9, are approved as a 10-hour continuing education take-home text book by the Florida Department of Professional Regulation (Board of Architecture and Interior Design), course reference number 02.03.093 for Florida licensed Interior Designers.

10 9 8 7 6 5 4 3 2 1

Book sellers may order this book in bulk quantities at a discounted price for resale to the general public. Contact the publisher.

Illustrations by Jeffrey W. Verheyen.
Cover design by Pat Cross.
Typesetting by Gallery Graphics
in Aster and Helvetica typefaces.
Printing by Rose Printing.

Durwood Publishers
Box 37474
Tallahassee FL
32315-7474

ISBN 0-927412-02-0

contents

preface

The timing is right! Never before has so much attention been paid to kitchens and baths. National magazines are devoted to these spaces. Regional housing publications hold kitchen- or bath-design contests. Newspapers cannot get enough photos and feature articles about them. A design-association chapter is selling kitchen and bath templates to raise money like a bake sale. Is this subject popular, or what?

Now, kitchens and baths have magnificent choices of style and products that can indulge adequately or amply. Manufacturers have made it possible to bring an array of traditional styles into a kitchen or a bath. Likewise, contemporary styles can be expressed with distinctive differences, not cookie-cutter similarities.

During this revolution, several associations asked me to present full-day workshops on kitchen and bath lighting. I did. I went from the East Coast to the West Coast and into Canada, covering seventeen cities in three years. What a focus! It was unlike any other I had experienced in years of presenting lighting programs. Associations previously requested many different lighting topics. Something must be special about kitchen and bath lighting. There is. First, these spaces, particularly baths, are hard to light. At the same time, these spaces demand good lighting so that the tasks can be seen easily and the visual environment can be the most attractive for the money spent. Second, lighting information is hard to obtain. A publication or central source containing all the facts needed to plan such lighting does not exist. Third, more attention is being paid to the lighting design of these spaces. At last!

The interior designers, certified kitchen and/or bath designers, lighting designers, certified showroom staff, architects, contractors, and electrical engineers in my workshops indicated how important this topic is. But they felt that their options were limited. Many have clients who want to remodel and are willing to spend money. Many have clients who want to build and get more bells and whistles than ever before. In addition, many workshop participants want to use the information for themselves, knowing first hand the value of good lighting in both kitchens and baths.

Contrary to popular belief, information is abundant but not obvious, and options are plentiful but not always readily available. Consequently, I decided that the information and the options should be brought together in a book. It is intended to be a how-to book on lighting for design professionals, installers, and homeowners.

In addition, it is intended to be a continuing-education text book. In states with mandatory continuing-education requirements for relicensing, practicing interior designers lack opportunities to complete their requirements at home. This lack is particularly a problem for those who can not leave home. This seemed unfair to me. Hence, I decided that if I could not get someone else to do something about it, I would. I could not; so I did! This book was reworked to be interactive, requiring the reader to get involved in the information and make discoveries about lighting. For continuing-education credits, the text book is accompanied by a work booklet that is mailed back to the publisher.

Lighting is a highly technical subject. This book can supply information for wisely choosing between many options, but it can not make the reader a specialist in lighting. A lot more training is required. Further, lighting uses electricity, which can be harmful. Consequently, the author and publisher take no responsibility for the reader's interpretations and/or uses of the material contained herein. In addition, using a qualified electrician for installation is strongly advised.

Lighting necessitates thoughtful planning because the end product is seen. It continues to be seen until the lighting is remodeled or the building is demolished. Lighting fixtures last longer than kitchen countertops or bathroom wallpaper. Consequently, the money invested in good lighting continues to pay back for a long time.

The two-hundred and nineteen illustrations in the book are intended to make memorable educational points and might not necessarily represent light as it actually looks in a space. They are intended to instruct by showing where light is coming from and where it goes first.

Jeff Verheyen graciously agreed to draw the additional illustrations needed for this book to add to the high-quality drawings he did for my first book: *LIGHT, LIGHT, LIGHT*.

Some technical illustrations from manufacturers are included, which show educational points better than we could. Some illustrations were inspired by manufacturers' elegant products. Thanks! Additional thanks go to Alice Fisher for proofing, to Moses Rodin at Gallery Graphics for excellent typesetting, and to Randy Demarco, my account executive at Rose Printing.

With the knowledge of what is possible, informed decisions can be made by those who want to specify the most desirable lighting environment possible. Such lighting will be beneficial in the many ways for many years. I hope you enjoy working with this book; I have enjoyed writing it.

chapter

what are your options for electric lighting?

What are your options as a designer for electric lighting in kitchens and baths? They are almost limitless. The technology of lighting is full of choices and the art of lighting is resplendent with aesthetic decisions. The technology responded to the federal government's call to conserve energy with low energy consumption of light sources and highly efficient fixtures. But not all of the technically improved choices hang in your local lighting showrooms. Some reside in the lighting catalogs or can be built-in.

The art of lighting responded to the increased public demand for aesthetics and different style choices. But not all of the styles hang in your local lighting showrooms. Some reside in lighting catalogs and others reside in furniture showrooms, antique shops, and import stores.

Within a kitchen and bath, the designer has the option to light what should be seen, because light demands attention, capturing the eye. Therefore, never light anything you do not want seen.

Color awakens with light. Light can create intoxicating highlights and distinctive shadows. Light and shadow can create pleasing patterns.

See for Yourself #1: Light Captures the Eye

At night, turn out all the lights except one in a room. Turn out all the lights in adjacent rooms or hallway. Reenter the room with one light. Observe what you look at first when reentering.

Light enhances the apparent value of objects, like a sorcerer's alchemy. Light makes details visible, almost magnifying them for view.

See for Yourself #2: Light Seems to Magnify

Take a phone book to a dimly lit closet. Observe the difficulty or ease of reading the numbers. Take the same phone book to a sunny window or an area of direct electric light and observe the difficulty or ease of reading the numbers.

Further, light can create a mood or evoke a feeling—soothing or stimulating. It is the fragrance for the visual senses. With different systems, light can create multiple moods with a fingertip touch to a programmable dimmer.

Light has the power to match colors exactly or mismatch definitely. Light can enhance or diminish people's productivity, even in the home.

See for Yourself #3: Light Creates Highlights

Take a set of metal dining utensils (knife, fork, spoon) into an unlit bathroom during the day. Put them down on a shelf or countertop. Observe the highlights, if any, on the metal. Then, take the same utensils to a sunny surface or surface lighted with direct, bright electric light. Observe the highlights.

Designers who specify lighting—lighting consultants, interior designers, architects, electrical engineers, and others—have not made a dent in the endless possibilities of lighting. These specifiers are faced with ever changing light sources, adding, not subtracting, from the choices; with many fixtures that come in and go out quickly; and with custom-built lighting that requires perseverance to accomplish. In addition, the information about lighting is fragmented and difficult to obtain.

Lighting choices are further complicated by codes aimed at several goals, including the excellent goal of saving energy. In an effort to accomplish this goal, some of the codes end up being unnecessarily restrictive. In addition, code enforcement is uneven.

Lighting is so complicated that many specifiers repeat their past designs. This practice ignores the new choices. Other specifiers abdicate their responsibility and let the contractor or installer (electrician) make the choices. This practice gives us poor luminous environments.

See for Yourself #4: Light Creates Shadow

Take a bookend or other solid vertical object and place it on a surface in front of a plain, pale-colored wall. Shine a flashlight on the bookend. Observe the lightness or darkness of the shadow on the wall. Take a brighter light (bright flashlight, directional-light desk lamp, or auto trouble light) and shine it on the bookend. Observe the darkness or lightness of the shadow as compared to the previous one.

To make good lighting design choices, the specifier must skillfully interweave client's needs, perceptual likes and dislikes, the sensory experience of the space, and the least energy consumption for the lighting required.

Tasks in a kitchen or bath require visual information to be accomplished. Designers need to know how frequent the task is performed, where, and what time of day if accessible to daylight. Each task has an optimal lighting condition. Basic lighting principles apply to choosing lighting for the task.

Nontask lighting in kitchens and baths provides the visual clarity, balance, highlight, shadow, pattern, color emphasis, rhythm, and line. It defines shape and mass. Among other things, nontask lighting can be brilliant rather than bland. It can be diverse rather than dull. It can expand or confine the space. It can enhance or diminish texture. Use these visual tools.

Light what you and your client want to see in a way that suits the client's lifestyle. Most lighting design is not produced by determining what is desirable to be seen. It should be. Most lighting design is produced by choosing fixtures. Instead, light distribution should be chosen. Hence, think of lighting design in a new way—where is light seen?

Light task surfaces first.

light is seen in two places

Where is light seen? It is seen reflecting from a surface or seen at the source (a bare light bulb), if visible. Light is not seen in the air! We think the air is lighted because so many surfaces reflect and rereflect light. The reflections and rereflections illuminate a space. Surfaces to be lighted can be task surfaces, such as kitchen desktops. Or surfaces can be nontask surfaces, such as ceilings and walls. Visible sources can be bare lamps (light bulbs) in a chandelier or lamp faces in an open ceil-

ing downlight. Fixture parts that appear bright are surfaces that are reflecting light. (For example, a louver lets some light through, which cannot be seen, and reflects other light at different angles on the surface of the louver, which can be seen.) Overall, we can see light on an illuminated desktop and we can also see light at bare lamps in a chandelier. The best options for lighting kitchens and baths are to light the surfaces you want seen and to include visible sources if they add to the ambience.

Visible sources can be bare lamps in a chandelier.

Unwanted visible sources can be lamps showing in shallow fixtures.

task surfaces

Task surfaces should be the first surfaces to be lighted. Task surfaces can be defined as surfaces where a visual task will take place. A kitchen countertop is a task surface. In addition, directions on a pizza mix box is also a task surface. The pizza box might not be lying flat on the kitchen countertop, but it needs

light to be visible to the cook. Task surfaces are more than objects; they are also people. In kitchens, task surfaces are primarily objects. In baths, task surfaces are primarily people. The face at a mirror is a task surface. The mirror is not the task surface. The mirror is the place where the task surface is seen.

Mirrors should not be lighted; faces should be. Likewise, colors are judges in bathroom mirror. Hence, true colors need to be seen.

In kitchens or baths, contrast of task details and task background is necessary to make tasks visible. (A small brown bug in oatmeal would be difficult to see; whereas the same small brown bug in Cream of Wheat would be more easily seen.) Also, some tasks require seeing the form and depth of an object. (Cutting tasks need lighting from an angle to enhance depth perception.)

Kitchen Task Surfaces

- countertops
- items inside cabinets
- eating top
- stove top
- desktop
- sink
- reading materials
- inside major appliances
- major room surfaces

In residences, designers will find it difficult to predict exactly where object task surfaces (pizza boxes) might be. In commercial structures, object task surfaces are more predictable. In residences, people task surfaces can be predicted with knowledge of clients' needs and lifestyle. (For example, does your client shave with an electric razor walking around the house or does he shave in front of a mirror?) These decisions are not unchangeable, but with up-to-date information, you can design task surfaces for present needs, and in five years you may be asked to redesign as needs and lifestyles change.

Major appliance manufacturers usually provide lighting inside appliances (refrigerators, freezers, ovens, and wine chillers) for object tasks. Designers can provide the rest.

Bath surfaces must be lighted by designers. Task lighting uses light's ability to make details and colors visible so that the task target (whiskers, for example) contrasts with the task background (the skin).

Task lighting can be switched at the task or at the door. The light fixtures providing the illumination for task surfaces might not necessarily be the first accessible wall switch at the door. Typically, the first accessible switch controls general light, rather than task light. But this practice is not a rule. In kitchens, the light for countertops could be the first accessible switch, particularly where many countertops are lighted and the surface color is highly reflective and could provide some general illumination.

Bath Task Surfaces

- faces at mirrors
- bodies in shower and tub
- countertops
- inside cabinets
- reading material (wherever located)
- steps
- major room surfaces for cleaning

nontask surfaces

Accent Surfaces

Accent surfaces may or may not be lighted. Accent light can add to the general illumination. In addition, lighted accents enrich a room and give it visual variety. Accent surfaces can be small or large where light is intended to highlight and attract attention. For example, accent surfaces can be items on a tabletop (vase of fresh flowers) or a grouping of furniture (a loveseat and coffee table).

In residences, designers specify the interior furnishings and finishes that can be accent surfaces. Hence, designers can predict where future decorative objects might be placed within the space and provide light for them. In commercial spaces, predicting is more difficult since designers usually do not work with the end user.

Accent Surfaces

- furniture tops or fronts
- furniture (eating table or conversation area)
- artwork
- plant materials
- decorative objects (freestanding or on tabletops)

Accent light can increase the brilliance of surface colors. It can reveal greater detail, put on highlights, and create shadows. The lighting designer controls these options. Accent light adds visual variety. It is a good tool for creating a specific mood or controlling what is seen. Use it!

Lighting fixtures for accent surfaces should not be the first accessible wall switch, because the amount of light is usually small and highly confined.

Wall Surfaces

Special walls deserve light. Light on the wall enhances the visual environment and justifies the expense of the special wall covering. Equally important, the light reflects back into the space for additional general illumination. Pattern, texture, or a special color on the wall should be lighted to make it visible at night. Illuminate such walls by either washing or grazing. Pattern and color can be wall washed with fixtures up to 4 feet back from the wall. Texture should be grazed with fixtures as close to the wall as possible.

WALL WASHING

Wall washing is light washing down a wall with fixtures at least 1½ feet back from the wall. Washing utilizes light's ability to attract attention and makes colors more visible. The decorative impact is light on a wall, softly reflecting into the space. Walls can be washed with light with two visual impacts at the top of the wall: with or without scallops. With scallops, the beams create a row of arches near the ceiling. Some people hate the arches; others tolerate them.

Most fixtures make scallops; some are well engineered to wash smoothly. Wall-washing fixtures are ceiling recessed or surface mounted. Adjustable fixtures help the designer fine tune the lighting on site. The most adjustable are, of course, track fixtures. But if surface mounted, they also are the most visible. Tracks can be recessed into custom-built ceiling troughs or purchased as manufactured troughs, elegantly engineered. The adjustability of recessed fixtures varies. Be

Do not wash a painted wall;...

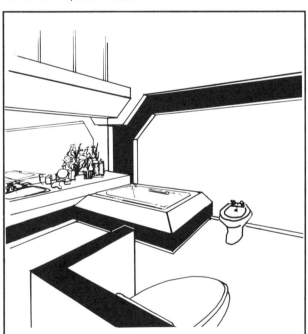

...otherwise, plastering flaws are revealed.

sure to check technical information about the fixtures under consideration. The best visual impact is the wall lighted with no fixtures in view.

Without scallops, the light makes an even wash. Only well-engineered fixtures produce even light. Reflectors or lenses are required to spread the light. Some designers insist on wall light without scallops. The wall covering can dictate whether scallops would disadvantage the wall. If the features or details on the wall would conflict with scallops, wash the wall without scallops. For example, on the one hand, a plaid wallpaper with lighting scallops at the top creates a conflicting pattern. On the other hand, plain wallpaper would probably not be offensive with a row of carefully placed lighting scallops.

Wall Washing Do's and Don'ts

- Do not wash a painted wall; otherwise all plastering flaws are revealed.
- Do not wash a polished marble, glossy tiled, or mirrored wall; otherwise spots of glare appear.
- Do wash a wall covered with:
  -wallpaper
  -wood paneling
  -fabric.
- Do filter the ultraviolet light rays for walls covered with materials that you want to save for the next generation—handpainted murals, tapestries, etc.

Position wall-washing fixtures at least 1½ feet away from the wall. The actual distance depends upon the height of the ceiling and the ability of the fixture to light the wall. If the fixtures are too far back, the light will start part way down the wall. The light should start at the ceiling. Even spacing of the fixtures is required for even distribution and even scallops. The distance between the fixtures and beam spread of the lamps determine the width of the scallops—the further apart the fixtures, the wider the scallops. Usually the first fixture is positioned in from the edge of the wall

at a distance that is one half the distance between the fixtures. Divide the length of the wall evenly and put one division in halves at each end. (This calculation is similar to determining the distance between drapery pleats.)

WALL GRAZING

Wall grazing is light skimming down a wall to enhance the texture with fixtures close to the wall. Any textured wall—masonry, rough sawn wood, textured wallpaper—should be grazed with light. The decorative impact is a lighted wall revealing shadows under the texture. The brighter the light, the darker the shadows. Some narrow scallops will occur at the top of the wall because of the position of the fixtures. Fixtures should be mounted less than 1½ feet from the wall and as close together as possible; the closer, the less scalloping. Constraints are the available space in the ceiling (plenum) for recessing and the cost of the fixtures for the purchaser. Adjustable fixtures are not required, because the light is aimed straight down. Fixtures can be recessed or surface mounted. Recessed fixtures create the most pleasing visual effect by not distracting from the view. Tracks can be used in custom-built or manufactured troughs.

Wall Grazing Do's and Don'ts

- Do not graze a polished marble, glossy tiled; or mirrored wall; otherwise, streaks of glare appear.
- Do position the fixtures as close together as you can afford.
- Do position the fixtures as close to the wall as possible, regardless of how close together.
- Do use incandescent sources, not fluorescent (too shadow free).

Wall lighting—washing or grazing—could be the first available switch at the door, since it could provide low-level general illumination.

general surfaces

General surfaces in a space can be lighted. These surfaces need light for cleaning. This function is more important in commercial

spaces than in residential. In commercial spaces, cleaning is a daily task; in residences, it is usually weekly. General surfaces are large surfaces (a ceiling or a row of cabinets) intended to reflect light throughout the kitchen and bath. Such surfaces do not need light if the total of all the other lighting distributions (task, accent, and wall) is sufficient. Otherwise, light large room surfaces to increase the general illumination.

General Surfaces

- large architectural surfaces:
  -ceilings
  -floors
  -walls
  -dividers
- continuous cabinets

General surface lighting should be the first accessible switch for the room. In California, the Energy Commission limits the type of light sources allowable for general illumination. Essentially, only fluorescent sources are acceptable. (The state specifies that lamps used in kitchens shall provide no less than 40 lumens per watt and in baths with the toilet shall have at least one fixture with lamps no less efficient than 40 lumens per watt.)

The need for general lighting has given rise to the overuse of a center-ceiling light as the only fixture in kitchens and baths. A center-ceiling light does not light tasks. It casts a person's shadow on the task. A center-ceiling distribution makes it difficult to see details. General illumination is second in priority to task lighting. But most often, a center-ceiling light is expected to do the complete job. It cannot.

Likewise, a chandelier only—the historical method of general lighting—creates either glare when facing the chandelier or dimness when facing away; neither is good.

visible sources

Besides being reflected from a surface, light can also be seen at a visible source—typically a bare lamp in a visible fixture or a candle in a candelabra. Both can be charming when they give soft light. The designer should plan when and where to have visible sources.

Visible Sources for Tasks

- bare-lamp chandelier with downlight
- transparent wall sconce
- transparent pendant
- ceiling-mounted surface fixture with bare lamps
- linear incandescent lamps
- G lamps on a channel

Sometimes visible sources appear but were not expected. Unplanned ones are most often an illuminated lamp in a shallow recessed fixture. The circles of illumination on the ceiling were not intended but are very apparent. Usually it is too late to change to deeper recessed fixtures that hide the lamp at a 45-degree viewing angle. Shallow plenums in new construction (some only 6 inches deep) prevent choosing deep recessed fixtures. Consider using horizontal-mounted compact fluorescent or small R20 incandescent downlights to avoid bright lamp faces being unplanned visible sources. Plan visible sources well; they are always in view.

Clear or coated, candelabra or medium base, and line or low voltage are some of the options for visible sources. Further, many shapes are available, enhancing a traditional fixture in a traditional way or enlivening a contemporary fixture in a new way. Consider all the options before choosing.

Visible fixtures not for tasks are lighting jewelry. Jewelry is wonderful but it does not replace task lighting. If wiring is installed, lighting jewelry can be hooked up at a later time. Although, most often, clients buy lighting jewelry first, it should come last. Purchase it after the other lighting is satisfactorily completed.

Visible Sources for Decoration

- bare-lamp chandelier
- translucent pendant
- low-voltage tube and string lights
- low-voltage bare-wire with MR and T lamps
- neon
- cold cathode
- channels with G, T, or S lamps
- ceiling-mounted surface fixture with bare lamps

distributions

Whether sources are seen or unseen light distributed can be uniform or nonuniform. Uniform spreads light fairly evenly throughout the kitchen or bath. Consequently, light at a task location (kitchen countertop, for example) would be the same amount as in the middle of the floor where it is not needed. Uniform light distribution is not appropriate for kitchens and baths. Why light the center of the floor at the same level needed for countertops? No reason. The visual effect of uniform lighting is bright from wall to wall. The lighting is bland. Energy is consumed at places that do not need light. Uniform lighting does not permit creativity.

Nonuniform distribution lights some places brighter than others. Consequently, a task location could be lighted at a level suitable for the age of the occupant and for the difficulty of the task. Other areas of the kitchen could have no direct light at all but receive reflected light. The visual effect of nonuniform is some areas bright and some dim. Nonuniform lighting uses the ability of light to capture attention and to reveal details of the task. The space appears diverse and interesting. Tasks are effectively lighted. Energy is consumed where it is needed. Options for choosing the many lighting possibilities are almost limitless with nonuniform distribution. Keep your design options open; do not limit them with uniform lighting. Nonuniform lighting can be creative and can be more interesting and varied.

Uniform lighting.

Wilsonart

Nonuniform lighting.

Wilsonart

fixtures

Fixture choices for the designer are almost endless, but they are not constant. Manufac-turers quickly drop fixtures that do not sell. Over the years, I have liked certain fixtures and hoped that I could ultimately get a client that would like them also, only to find that they had been discontinued. The marketplace rules availability. Designers need to have access to many current catalogs. (Compact disks hooked up to computers can replace shelves of catalogs for computer-literate designers.)

Fixture choices are visible fixtures or not-so-visible fixtures. The options for the designer

Skylights with electric light sources can illuminate general surfaces.

are: to purchase ready-made fixtures (pendants, wall sconces, low-voltage tubes), to custom-build architectural fixtures (canopies, soffits, coves), or for the brave designer, to custom-build visible fixtures (chandeliers, pendants, surface-mounted).

All fixtures should have a safety-approval label (like a UL label). It assures that the fixture conforms to the national safety standards. Most local codes require these standards. Custom-made fixtures should conform to safety standards also, but approval is difficult and time-consuming to get. Custom-made fixtures are for the brave designer with the time and patience to get such approval. The consequences of unsafe fixtures are not worth the risk.

Style in a kitchen or bath can be set by the style of a visible fixture. Or the style of the kitchen or bath can be followed when choosing a visible fixture. Visible fixtures are like jewelry. Often, jewelry for clothing is chosen before the clothes. Other times, the clothes are purchased and then accessorized with jewelry. The same thing happens with lighting fixtures. For both ways, the choice of options is driven by aesthetics, a worthy motivator. But complete the lighting of the space with additional lighting sources.

Not-so-visible, custom-built architectural fixtures can deliver light with the least light-source recognition. They clearly integrate well into any style kitchen or bath. The designer who wishes to incorporate custom-made, architectural fixtures needs to be in the decision-making process early. The earlier the better. More options are available for the designer early in the process.

energy choices

The designer has not only the option of line voltage or low voltage but also how much energy the lighting design will consume now and forever. Opt for energy-efficient choices, even in states that do not regulate lighting choices for energy savings. Everyone benefits.

Simple calculations can be made to offer the client choices for how much energy they want to consume over the lifetime of the lighting design. An inexpensive fixture and lamp that consumes more energy will cost more in the long run. Energy-conserving fixtures and lamps that initially might be expensive will cost less in the long run. Help con-

serve our unrenewable resources by choosing the energy-efficient options.

The designer has options for controlling the lighting with switches and dimmers. Programmable dimmers provide the most options for control. They are excellent for kitchens and can be suitable for high-end baths. Dimmers are not an energy-conserving tool; they are a scene-making tool.

Overall, lighting has more options than any other interior design component, but lighting demands understanding the technology and is more difficult to change once installed. Choose the options wisely!

chapter

2

process of lighting design

Usually, lighting is planned last in the building design process. At that point, little money is available to spend on electric lighting. Moreover, the time for architecturally designing daylighting is long gone. Opportunities are lost and options are reduced.

Further, professional lighting advice is not used. To complicate matters, worthy examples of good kitchen and bath lighting to copy are scarce. Consequently, one or more of the deadly sins of lighting design are committed.

Seven Deadly Sins of Lighting Design

1. Visual image of space not considered.
2. Fixtures chosen for aesthetic reasons only.
3. Built-in lighting choices ignored.
4. Bias against fluorescent sources perpetuated.
5. Only one type of lighting distribution used.
6. Daylighting not controlled or amplified.
7. Glare created.

For the most part, the usual design process is choosing ready-made visible fixtures—chandeliers and other surface-mounted lighting equipment. Chandeliers and other decorative

Visible fixtures are jewelry.

fixtures are lighting jewelry. They are designed to be beautiful, but alone they cannot create a good lighting environment. Surface-mounted equipment (center-ceiling fixtures, etc.) can be both exceedingly utilitarian and too bright. They usually do not create a good lighting environment either. Normally, built-in custom-made lighting is not even considered. The decision to build in must be made early in the design process. Consequently, lighting designers should be involved in the beginning, not just at the end.

optimal design process

The optimum lighting design process is to design the lighting at the same time the kitchen or bath is planned. For the greatest amount of options, the designer should have input in the structural decisions of walls, ceiling, cabinets, and finishes.

Likewise, expenditures for electric lighting should be generous since lighting lasts a long time and remodeling lighting is costly. Lighting should cost, at the least, four percent of the cost of the kitchen or bath, including architecture, fixtures, and finishes. Kitchens and baths are regularly the most expensive spaces in a residence. Poorly lighted kitchens and baths do not function well. Conse-quently, spending enough money to get good lighting is important.

Optimum lighting design should provide more than one type of lighting distribution. For example, avoid only downlight; combine uplight, downlight, and general diffused light.

Optimum lighting design should provide more than one lighting system. A lighting system is a single fixture or a series of fixtures controlled together. For example, cove fixtures above the upper kitchen cabinets separately switched is a system. Likewise, an illuminated skylight on a switch is a system. On a programmable dimmer, several systems can be combined on one dimmer and several dim-

Optimum lighting design should provide…

…more than one lighting system.

St. Charles

St. Charles

mers combined on one switch for one scene. Programmable dimmers permit additional levels of lighting options and creativity unequalled by any other control device.

Optimum lighting design should be thought of in visual terms. Decide what the visual impression of the kitchen or bath should be and what should be lighted. Tasks are the first priority. General illumination is second and can be provided by task, wall, and accent lighting combined. Finally, decorative fixtures, if any, are the last priority. Hopefully, they can be included because, as jewelry, they add brilliance and style and can enliven the space.

Optimum lighting design should include a detailed examination of which surfaces should be lighted. Surface finishes should be known, because color (dark or pale) and finish type (gloss or matte) are critical to lighting. Dark colors absorb light. Glossy finishes can create glare or an unwanted reflection of a bare lamp. For example, glossy backsplashes can reflect bare-lamp, under-cabinet lighting like a mirror. The designer will want to choose sources and fixtures with surface finishes in mind.

Likewise, the visual effect of the surfaces that will receive light and the visible fixtures should be judged. Remember, the lighting design will last a long time.

After deciding what surfaces should be lighted, then decide how bright these surfaces should be. Remember from *See For Yourself #1*, the brightest surfaces will attract attention. Also, remember task light needs to be bright enough to reveal details of the task for the age of the person and for the speed and accuracy required. The older the person is, the more light is needed. The more difficult the details are to see, the more light is needed.

Task Details

Difficult	Easy
■ small size	■ large size
■ minimal contrast with background	■ maximal contrast with background
■ speed and accuracy needed	■ speed and accuracy not required

Small details with minimal background contrast are the most difficult to see. If the light falls on a glossy surface (glossy cooking magazine) and the angle of the light is such that it produces a glare (reflected into the eye of the viewer), easy task details become difficult. Unfortunately, many factors affect visibility.

Finally, speed and accuracy require bright light. Usually speed and accuracy are not life threatening in kitchens and baths (they are in medical facilities). Accuracy does affect health and safety in kitchens and baths. Sharp instruments are used in both spaces. Likewise, clean versus dirty can affect health in the kitchen; it affects image in the bath.

Correct identification of foreign objects (like bugs) in food can affect health (or is it just more protein, like some glibly say). Bright light from the optimum direction with optimum receiving surfaces help identification. Inaccurate visual information due to poor lighting can be a disadvantage.

The reality of how bright a lighted surface will appear is affected by the color of that surface. Dark colors absorb more light than pale colors.

See for Yourself #5: Color Affects Reflection of Light

If you have a photo light meter or a camera with a built-in light meter, point the meter toward a piece of white paper in direct sunlight. Read the dial. Also, point the meter toward a black book cover or black construction paper in direct sunlight. Read the dial. Which reads higher reflected light?

Photometer.

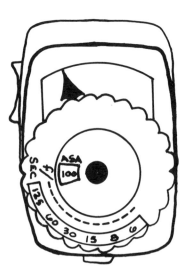

How bright a lighted surface will appear is affected by the distance from the light and the angle of the light. Light falling straight to the surface will be the brightest. Likewise, the further the source is away from the surface, the less light there will be.

How Distance Affects Light

Light decreases by the square of the distance.
Footcandles = candlepower ÷ distance^2

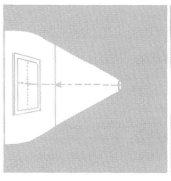 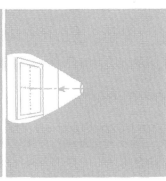

The farther the source, the less light.

The closer the source, the more light.

Also, surfaces perpendicular to the light source receive the most light. Surfaces at an angle receive less light. Light from downlights to tabletop or floor surfaces at an angle needs to be calculated with modification of the cosine of that angle. Light from downlights on wall surfaces needs to be calculated with modification of the sine of the angle.

How Angle Affects Light

Footcandles = candlepower @ ∠ x cosine or sine of ∠

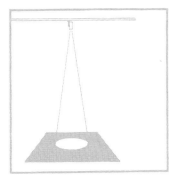 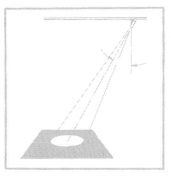

Surfaces perpendicular to the source receive the most light.

Surfaces at an angle receive less light.

How bright a lighted surface will appear when ceiling downlights are used is affected by the geometry of the space. Light from a downlight in small, tall rooms is more likely to strike the walls and/or tall cabinets and be absorbed. Downlight in large, 8-foot ceiling rooms is less likely to strike the walls and/or tall cabinets and be absorbed, thereby getting down to task or other surfaces that should be bright.

Downlight in small, tall rooms is usually absorbed by the walls.

Downlight in large, 8-foot-ceiling rooms is not usually absorbed by the walls.

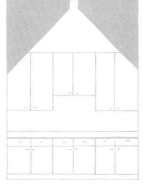 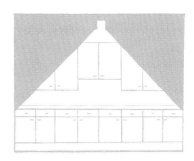

Shadows define the shape of objects and reveal texture. Shadows can be produced by light. Frequently, shadows are ignored in the design process. Not good! To reveal deeply carved cabinets or furniture, use light to create shadows. To reveal highly textured fabrics or finishes, use light. To create shadow patterns on smooth surfaces, use light projected through filigree lenses, open woodwork or plant materials.

Shadows have hard or soft edges. The brighter the light is, the harder the edges and the darker the value of the shadows. For example, in bright sunlight, shadows are very sharp and dark. Under cloudy skies, shadows are indistinct and pale. Likewise, shadows closest to the object casting the shadow are the sharpest and darkest. For another example, at the bottom of a flagpole on a sunny day, the shadow is distinct. Farther along the ground, the shadow is less distinct, due to additional light reflecting from the sky. Moreover, direct electric light creates the sharpest, darkest shadows. Indirect light creates indistinct and pale shadows, if any at all. Use shadows in interiors to enliven and enhance.

Frequently, direct light reflections are ignored in the design process. However, reflections can create sparkle, if they are small and subtle. Choose reflections wisely. Baths with glossy surfaces (ceramic lavatories, polished stone knobs, or shiny metal faucets) and surfaces of water cascading from waterfall faucets into deep tubs offer opportunities to create sparkle. Kitchens with shiny silverware, crystal, and other tabletop objects offer additional opportunities. (I like to create reflections onto the ceiling above a table from direct light on gold place mats and brass charger plates. Some people never notice, but the glitter, nonetheless, is there for the eyes of the beholder.) Remember, the difference between sparkle and glare is size. Sparkle is small; glare is large.

Light reflected from a neutral colored surface carries no apparent color, just light. If light is reflected from an intensely colored surface, a tint of the color is reflected, wanted or unwanted. (One of my students at Florida State University did his master's thesis art show by reflecting light from one painting to another, to yet another. Subtle, but elegant!)

Ceilings in interiors are usually ignored. Yet, outdoors, the sky is the primary source of light and changing colors. John Constable, an English painter, noted that the light of the sky governed everything. To this point, in traditional French-style interiors, artists paint trompe l'oeil skies on ceilings to recreate the visual excitement of the sky indoors. With cleverness, use ceilings for reflected washes of light, even with subtle color changes.

Also, a smooth surface of water in a tub can be like a mirror and reflect a brightly lighted perpendicular surface adjacent to it. Create such a scene if the tub is viewed from a distance, especially from another room.

Optimum lighting design can create a mood or atmosphere in the space. A soothing mood is associated with lighting below eye level with hidden sources and low amounts of warm colored light. Consequently when designing a soothing scene, keep lighting below eye level with hidden sources and low amounts of warm colored light. Use any of the not-so-visible fixtures and do not use blue-white light. Dimmed, incandescent, either line-voltage low-wattage or low-voltage, or warm fluorescent are best. By the same token, the light can be well spread, if soft, or can be confined to a small intimate area.

By contrast, a stimulating mood is associated with bright, broadly distributed cool colored light, often with visible sources. Consequently, when designing for a lively atmosphere, put visible, bare lamps in sight, par-

With large expanses of glass…

…at night, windows go black.

ticularly many small ones. Low-voltage incandescent light in small bright spots with tubes, strings, or on bare wires create brilliance and are small. Further, use wall and/or ceiling light. Light should be well spread from visible, but not glaring, or hidden sources. Determine what sources need to be seen and what sources can be hidden.

Research at Penn State in the Architectural Engineering Department indicates that feelings of privacy are reinforced by nonuniform light distribution with low amounts near the person and higher amounts farther away. Some cooks may prefer such a feeling when cooking. Some people in the bath might also.

The research also indicates that pleasure is reinforced by nonuniform lighting with emphasis on the walls. In kitchen eating areas, wall lighting could reinforce the enjoyment of the food. In baths, wall lighting could reinforce a leisurely soak in the tub.

Colors have an influence. In our culture, blue is accepted as creating a cool atmosphere. Red is accepted as creating a warm atmosphere. Use these accordingly. However, in Asian cultures, cool light is the most acceptable. Asians do not care for the effect of warm-color light on their skin. A suntanned appearance is not coveted as it is in our culture. Other cultures have other preferences. Design according to preference. Many colors of light are available to create the atmosphere desired.

Finally, fixture style also creates atmosphere. A fixture can set a mood that is carried out in the interior finishes and furnishings or can create a contrast to the interior style. Use style skillfully.

The optimum design process considers what happens to windows at night. They turn black, reflecting the inside space. The black windows reflect any direct light fixture (a lighted chandelier) and any brightly lighted surface (the ceiling with cove light). The reflection is distracting and can be glaring. Consequently, light the outdoors with suburban or rural low-rise structures where large expanses of glass are used in kitchens or baths. Additional light sources outside can balance the inside lighting and reduce the glare. The lighted outdoors becomes an extension of the indoor space, and if sufficiently bright, wipes away the glare. (In cities, outdoor light is provided by others, but the principles of direct light reflection applies, creating an unintended glare.)

In cities, outdoor light is provided by others.

How bright a lighted surface will appear is affected by the choice of light sources and fixtures. Well-engineered fixtures and lamps produce the greatest amount of light. Higher wattage from incandescent sources does not always mean more footcandles. Frequently, brightness from a high-wattage, line-voltage incandescent can be equalled by a low-wattage, low-voltage source. Designers should compare technical data of products before choosing. What is described as the same, indeed, may not be.

Fixtures chosen must integrate into the construction and be accessible to electricity. Construction and electricity limit the options. For example, concrete and steel construction ceilings can only accept recessed fixtures if wiring and housings are included in the forming stage. Otherwise, surface fixtures and surface wiring are mandated.

Sloped or high ceilings influence choices of fixtures and sources. Sloped ceilings, for example, with recessed fixtures would deliver different amounts and beams of light with the same light source. The fixture farthest from the floor would deliver a wider, dimmer light. Use this difference in the design; otherwise, lamp the higher recessed fixtures with higher wattages. Also, adjustable recessed fixtures would be required to compensate for the ceiling slope. In contrast, pendants and other suspended fixtures easily compensate for sloped ceilings giving even illumination.

High ceilings hold surface-mounted ceiling fixtures out of view in average size rooms, thereby reducing the visual clutter (track fixtures, in particular). However, high ceilings permit seeing up into recessed fixtures, thereby requiring deeper housings. Also, fixtures must be large enough to hold higher wattage lamps to compensate for the light loss due to the distance.

Likewise, plenum depth dictates the depth of recessed fixtures. For example, a six-inch plenum eliminates eight-inch deep recessed fixtures. Sometimes plenums are deep, but electric access is not available—particularly in historic structures. Consequently, design with construction and electrical access in mind and save future disappointments. Positions of plumbing and heat/air ducts affect recessed lighting placement. Hopefully, the locations of these architectural necessities will be known early. Often they are not. Consequently, redesign becomes necessary.

Redesign requires the same careful consideration as the original design. Redesign is sometimes required when the final price of the lighting is determined. If so, purchase all built-in fixtures first. They are difficult to install later. Wire for future visible fixtures and purchase when affordable. When prewired, visible fixtures can be installed at any time. However, manufacturers frequently discontinue fixtures. Consequently, if a visible fixture is desirable because of its special style, waiting might be risky.

Sometimes redesign is required because a fixture cannot be shipped in time for the completion of the project. Allow six to eight weeks for fixture delivery. After designing, redesigning, ordering, and receiving, the lamps and fixtures need to be checked for accuracy. Substitutions are often made. Do not accept a substitute until you are satisfied that it is truly equal. Lamp substitutions are usually equal; fixtures are usually not.

Finally, optimal lighting design requires installing, lamping, and aiming. During the installation process, recessed fixtures might not be able to be placed where intended due to ceiling joints, heat/air duct, or unexpected plumbing locations. If so, carefully decide where the new location should be. If an incandescent downlight is used, the decision should include determining where the beam of light would fall in the space. Scallops of light misaligned with architectural features depreciate a good lighting design. Unintended blobs of bright light on architectural elements detract from the aesthetics.

Fixtures need to be lamped properly. Often recessed incandescent fixtures have internal adjustments to accept several different lamp sizes. Make sure the fixture is adjusted for the lamp chosen. Otherwise, light is wasted inside the fixture and efficiency is lost. Also, since incandescent recessed fixtures, both line and low voltage, accept different lamp sizes, your carefully chosen lamp should be in the correct fixture. On-site inspection is critical to assuring that the design gets carried to accurate completion.

Aiming lamps is the final step in the process. Aiming is required for all adjustable incandescent fixtures, recessed or surface mounted, particularly track lighting. Aim the light beam to the surface intended at the desired angle. Check to assure that no direct light-source glare is created, especially for stairs and seating areas. At stairs, glare can cause accidents. Solutions for glare are reaiming, installing a louver on the fixture, or increasing the amount of light in the space so that the brightness of the glare is diminished.

Information Needed for Lighting Designer

1. Time frame of job
2. Lighting deadlines
3. Construction type
4. Plenum depth and electrical access
5. Location of heat/air ducts and plumbing
6. End-user's needs and preferences
7. Money available for lighting
8. Latest lamps, fixtures, and controls
9. Interior finishes and colors
10. Furniture locations
11. Task location, details, and speed/accuracy required
12. Visual disabilities of end user

To assure that your special kitchen or bath lighting is maintained as planned, prepare a lamp-purchase chart for the owners. Such a chart enables the owners to continue to lamp the fixtures with correct lamps as they need replacements in the years to come. The chart should indicate what type of lamp should be used in each fixture and phone/address of supplier, if ordering is required. A well-designed lighting plan should be forever.

A Designer Needs To:

- Be awesome to the client (so they can't live without you).
- Become valued by the installer (defends your plan as a team member).
- Become ferocious with supplier (wouldn't dare substitute).
- Be there at lamping and aiming time (the make or break time).
- Prepare a lamp-purchase chart for clients (to assure that the lighting will be maintained).

Even though we adapt to most amounts of light without eye pain and even though we are not aware of its effects unless it is glaring or it is gone, light affects our ability to complete tasks, to see colors and textures, to have highlights and shadows, and to appear "in-the-best-light." Light has long-lasting importance for kitchens and baths. Once installed, the fixtures last for the life of the building or until taken down for remodeling. Unlike kitchen countertops or bathroom faucets, lighting fixtures are hardly ever replaced. Consequently, thoughtfully specify kitchen and bath electric lighting. Many choices are available and it will be used for a long time.

chapter

3

seeing light

Seeing is tricky. Light that enters the eye is sent as a nerve impulse to the brain. The eye/brain adapts to light and makes the best use of the information. Unless the person is disadvantaged in doing a visual task, available light seems sufficient. Most people fully adapt to available light in twenty minutes. The eyes can adapt to moonlight (about .01 foot-candles) or to bright sunlight at 10,000. This range is huge. Our eyes are probably the most adaptable part of our body. The adaptation process is affected by what the eye has previously adapted to. If, for example, a person is in a dimly lit room and goes to another dimly lit room, the person would probably feel that the light is sufficient. If, on the other hand, a person is in a dimly lit room and goes to a room that is a little brighter, the room would probably appear to be very bright. Consequently, the level of lighting in adjacent spaces to kitchens and baths affects the perception of the person entering the kitchen or bath.

In addition, how the eye/brain sees color is not constant. The color we see is influenced (either intensified or diminished) by the surrounding color. Also, the color we see is influenced by our memory of the correct color regardless of what our perception is at that moment. For example, in dim incandescent light a bright red tomato will actually look brownish-red, but our memory tells us that the tomato is bright red.

Color of light itself.

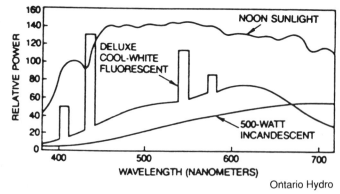

Ontario Hydro

Further, the color of the light itself affects the apparent color of surfaces it illuminates. For example, mercury lamps have a very narrow color range—blue—which distorts other colors. Consequently, a red car under mercury parking-lot lights would appear gray, and memory would not assist in the correct color identification.

Color of light and of surfaces affect color seen.

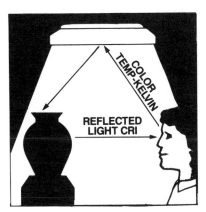

Sylvania

Light reflects color of the surface.

Sometimes interior finishes are disadvantaged by the color in light itself. For example, all white kitchens or baths with warm triphosphor fluorescent lamps (30°K) look peachy. Owners might be unhappy about losing the pristine white they chose for the floor, walls, and cabinets. (The National Kitchen and Bath Association reports that more than half of the baths and almost half of the kitchens installed are white.) Choose light sources carefully when lighting all white spaces. (See *Color of Fluorescent Light* and *How to Choose* in Chapter 4.)

The color in light affects matching samples. Unfortunately, color samples can appear to match under one light source, but mismatch under another. Therefore, always match color samples under the same light source (both electric and daylight) used in the space. The color of daylight is different at different locations and from different compass directions.

Sometimes interior finishes are disadvantaged by the reflected color of light. Intense colors on major surfaces that reflect light influence color of other surfaces. Light actually picks up the color of the first surface and reflects it. Consequently, the color on the secondary surface is altered. (This phenomenon is part of the reson that color of finish materials appears differently in the acutal space with other finish materials than the color appears in the studio or store.

Equally important, seeing light is a matter of being aware of and learning what to look for and responding to it. Awareness is a developed ability. Because of your training, you are probably able to see light better than your clients. You are likely to respond to how light reveals, models, and illuminates kitchens and baths. You must communicate this knowledge to your clients in order to sell them on lighting.

Light can inspire as well as reveal. Inspiration can come from light sparkling on water, animating a face, or creating a shadow pattern from latticework or leaves. Revealing can come from strong light on a multicolored patterned fabric, showing all its glory, which might be lost in dim light. Watercolor painters are masters of the ability to see and recreate light, particularly the Impressionists. Renoir, for instance, used light well on people's skin and white objects in the scenes. Monet was obsessed with light, using it to make large bulky objects almost dissolve. Further, the positioning of lighted areas and dark areas by watercolorists can teach lighting designers how to manipulate interior lighting. Studying watercolors will increase your ability to see light. Note the atmosphere effect that watercolorists create with their use of light. Some atmospheres are almost transparent; some are opaque. Likewise, interior lighting design can be the same.

Strong light affects the tonal value of interior furnishing and finishes. For example, a bright light on a pink sphere and on a red sphere creates a higher tonal value where the light strikes and a darker tonal shadow on the underside. The pink sphere, which is paler than the red sphere, could appear darker on underside areas than the brightly lighted top of the red sphere. Since light affects intensity of colors, a brightly lighted surface might appear more intense than intended in the color scheme. Or conversely, too much light could make surface color appear washed out. Too much light diminishes colors like an overexposed photograph. Light can intensify or diminish colors.

Because shapes, colors, values, and textures play on the eyes, the designer must isolate the variables into tones of pale to dark (that is why the illustrations in all my books are black line drawings with white for light and pale gray for shade). Artists do pencil studies with both pale and dark gray. This method defines shadows. If shadows are to be designed, use both grays; never use color. Color diverts the eye from looking at what is

Backlighting reveals outline of objects.

light and what is shade. A representation of the space with no color is called chiaroscuro. Rembrandt used chiaroscuro to achieve high-keyed paintings of people. Designers can use it to study scenes of light.

Moreover, seeing light is interpreted emotionally. For example, the interpretation of bright light is a high-keyed atmosphere, like a bright sunny beach with people and activities. The interpretation of dim light is a low-keyed atmosphere, like a starry night on the same beach with just two people strolling along.

The accuracy of seeing objects is affected by light. The way light falls on an object contributes largely to the image of its volume and solidity. The more light reveals visual information, the more the object will be viewed accurately. Both light and shadow generate this information—highlights on the top and deep shadows on underneath. On the one hand, light striking a solid object (freestanding furniture or kitchen object on a shelf) at 45° from the left or right brings about a strong impression of form and volume, particularly if a shadow is also seen. On the other hand, backlighting only gives information about the outline of the object. Likewise, light striking an object directly from the front gives little information about volume and solidity, because shadows are minimized and texture is flattened.

Even though the physical, intellectual, and emotional aspects of seeing light are unreliable, changeable, and adaptable, the effects of light are profound on interior spaces. Like a watercolor, a lighting design creates a scene forever.

chapter
4

lamps

The term "lamp" to lighting professionals means "light bulb." To everyone else, lamp means a light fixture that sits on a table (table lamp) or on the floor (floor lamp). What a mess! Since professionals in the field of lighting use the term lamp, lamp (or light source) is used in this book to mean light bulb and the term portable fixture to mean table, floor, or movable wall lamp.

Lamps can be divided into three categories: incandescent, discharge, and laser. Incandescent includes both line- and low-voltage tungsten filament (the light source used in table lamps) and halogen. Halogen is also called tungsten halogen or called quartz describing the glass enclosure. Low voltage needs a transformer to reduce the electrical power. Discharge lamps include fluorescent, both hot (standard fluorescent) and cold cathode, sodium, mercury, metal-halide, and neon. Discharge sources need a ballast to operate. Sodium, mercury, and metal-halide are also called high-intensity discharge, describing the pressure. Lasers require resonators and produce a narrow beam, single wavelength of light visible as one color.

Lamp Categories and Characteristics

Incandescent:
  line- or low-voltage
  halogen or nonhalogen
  point or linear source
  clear or coated glass

Discharge:
  fluorescent—
    linear or compact source
    self-ballasted or needing a ballast
    hot cathode or cold cathode

  sodium, mercury, or metal-halide—
    all point sources

  neon—
    linear

Laser:
  single wavelength

Incandescent and fluorescent are the most widely used for kitchens and baths. If your client lives in California, the energy code for new construction in kitchens and baths requires fluorescent sources (but does not permit screw-based fluorescent, since it can be replaced with incandescent).

Neon is not used for kitchen or bath task lighting, but it is unexcelled for decorative purposes. Lasers are totally decorative, requiring alcohol and water foggers to make the beam visible. High-intensity lamps—sodium, mercury, and metal-halide—are not used in kitchens or baths. However, new white sodium lamps in residential wattages are available and will be used in the future.

Thousands of different lamps are available in incandescent and fluorescent. But most people probably use only four or five in their residences. Other lamps are just waiting to be chosen. Many are old technology; others are new. Make use of both.

incandescent

Line Voltage

Incandescent lamps can be line voltage, usually 120 or can be low voltage, usually 12. Most line-voltage lamps are point sources. (Some are linear.) Point sources emit light from a small point rather than from a large surface. Point-source light can be easily controlled, making various beam widths—spot to flood. (Light from linear lamps is more difficult to control.) Point sources can produce distinctive shadows. Shadows enrich the visual environment. (Linear sources produce indistinctive shadows.)

The glass in the line-voltage incandescent lamps can be clear or coated. Clear lamps show the filament, which if not glaring can be sparkling. Coated lamps diffuse the light at the lamp. A special color-selective coating is available. It is dichroic. The dichroic coating permits only one hue to pass through, reflecting all others. Hence, the light augments a single color on the surface it strikes. The light cannot be seen on other color surfaces, including white. Blue dichroic lamps are used extensively by jewelry stores to heighten the blue background for diamonds. In kitchens and baths, the blue and the green dichroic together enrich plant materials or in other hues, punch up selected colors on surfaces for decorative reasons. Experiment with them; they are worth the trouble.

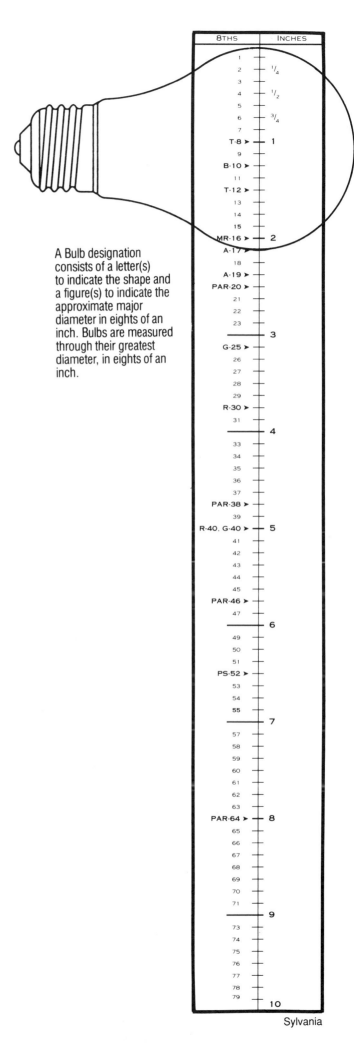

A Bulb designation consists of a letter(s) to indicate the shape and a figure(s) to indicate the approximate major diameter in eights of an inch. Bulbs are measured through their greatest diameter, in eights of an inch.

Sylvania

INCANDESCENT LAMPS

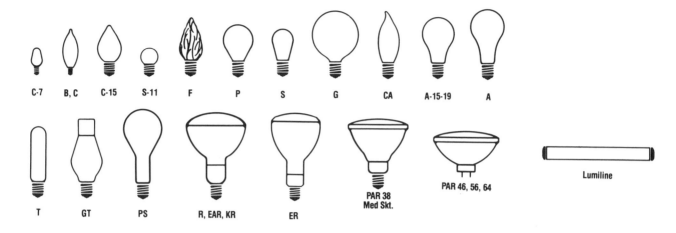

INCANDESCENT TUNGSTEN HALOGEN & QUARTZ LAMPS

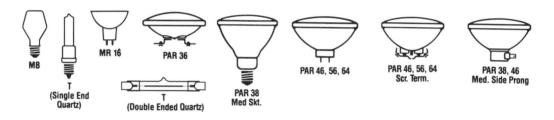

Sylvania

LAMPS FOR RECESSED OR TRACK FIXTURES

The most widely used line-voltage incandescent is the A lamp. It is available in 15 to 200 watts, with a rated life of 750 to 1,000 hours. Typically, if it cannot be seen, a coated (inside-frost) A lamp is used. However, a clear lamp can create interesting shadow patterns from an open downlight with a concentric baffle louver over the aperture. All A lamps are line voltage. They distribute light from all sides of the lamp. Consequently, they need fixture optics (reflectors, louvers, lenses) to control the light. They are inexpensive, but need frequent replacements, ending up costing more in the long run.

An A lamp can have a silvered bowl. The lamp is clear with a metallic coating on the face that reflects the light back into the reflector of the fixture. These lamps are widely used in Europe. They are usable in both recessed and track fixtures.

R (reflector) lamps are line voltage. They have a reflector inside the blown-glass envelope and produce a soft-edge beam of light. They are available in 25 to 500 watts with spot or flood beam widths. R lamps distribute the light from the face of the lamp. All have special distribution characteristics. Consult manufacturers' technical material for the latest specifics. Fixture optics can further control the beam of light. In fact, A lamps with parabolic reflectors in deep recessed fixtures can produce more footcandles than an R lamp in an open downlight at the same wattage. In addition, some Rs are made to produce heat; they are heat lamps. They are unexcelled in warming up a bathroom on a chilly evening before taking a shower, rather than heating the whole house with central heating. Consequently, they are energy efficient for the purpose of heating one room.

PAR (parabolic-aluminized reflector) lamps are either line or low voltage. The line-voltage version is considered an outdoor flood, but have applications indoors. Both have a reflector inside the pressed-glass envelope. They produce a distinct beam edge. They are available in 45 to 500 watts with many varieties of spot or flood beam widths. PARs also distribute the light from the face of the lamp. They can only be used in fixtures designed for them. Fixture optics can further control the beam. Like the R lamp, they are rated to last 2,000 hours. The newest PARs are halogen and have better light output, longer life, and excellent color. Use a 75-watt halogen PAR and expect to get the light that a standard 150-watt PAR would give. Over the life of the lamp, the energy savings would pay for the replacement.

ER (elliptical reflector) lamps are only line voltage. ERs deliver narrower beams than R or PAR floods, but wider beams than spots. The lamp is longer and needs a deep recessed fixture. It focuses the light two inches in front of the lamp and does not trap the light inside a deep recessed fixture. The 75-watt ER fits in 150-watt R or PAR fixtures. In many situations, the 75-watt ER gives as much light as needed. It delivers about the same amount as a 150-watt R but in a smaller area. In addition, the ER is available in a 150-watt size.

All R, PAR, and ER lamps burn hot at the base and must be used in porcelain or ceramic, not brass, sockets. Manufacturers list suitable lamps for the sockets in their fixtures. Follow their specifications.

All R, PAR, and ER lamps have specific beam spreads. Track-fixture manufacturers usually have beam-spread charts in their catalogs. Or lamp manufacturers can supply the technical data. Consult such data to design lighting.

HALOGEN LAMPS

Line- and low-voltage lamps can be halogen or nonhalogen. Halogen is incandescent. But unlike other incandescent, halogen gas is inside. Halogen lamp shapes can be MR, PAR, or T (tube); however, not all such shapes are halogen. Confusing, isn't it?

Halogens produce a whiter-appearing light. Nonhalogen lamps produce a creamy-colored light. Halogen sources can be smaller and more compact than nonhalogen, because they are well engineered.

The most widely used is the MR (multi-faceted reflector) lamp (MR16 or MR11). Some have a pressed-glass cover, like a PAR lamp; others have a small glass capsule in the middle of a reflector. Do not touch the MR without the pressed-glass cover with bare hands and choose a fixture with a lens to be safe.

Rule of Thumb for Safety with MR or T Lamps

Always handle a bare MR or T halogen lamp with gloves or a cloth. Otherwise, the oil from the fingers may cause the lamp to shatter when lit.

PAR halogen lamps are well engineered and can deliver light in many beam patterns and wattages, both line and low voltages. They last longer than standard PARs.

LAMPS FOR DECORATIVE FIXTURES

Many decorative shapes are available for decorative fixtures that show the lamp. If lamps are well chosen, they can flatter the fixture and the space. The list of shapes is long, but in most places the supply is short. Supplies are often clustered in big cities at electrical supply or lighting showrooms.

DECORATIVE LAMPS

C-7   S-11   B, C   C-15   F   CA   T   GT   PS   A   G   A-15-19   P   S

Sylvania

Chapter Four   **29**

Do not spoil an attractive chandelier or wall fixture with an indifferent lamp. Choose one that enhances it. Test the lamp in the fixture. Try several styles.

Manufacturers identify lamps by a letter and number coding. The letters indicate the shape. (The numbers indicate in eighths of an inch what the diameter of the lamp is at its widest point.) The teardrop, bent candle, and flame shapes (B, CA, and F) are the traditional shapes for bare-lamp chandeliers and wall fixtures. Some flame lamps are manufactured to flicker like a candle. However, these usually look better in restaurants than in residences.

The globe, teardrop, and cone shapes (G, B, and C) are good for stylized chandeliers. These nonflame shapes are different, not indifferent. They give an additional decorative look. Actually, G lamps, either line or low voltage, are used as bare lamps in linear channels. They are decorative points of light, as long as they are not glaring. Low voltage minimizes glare. In addition, silvered-bowl versions of G lamps reduce the glare potential when using high-wattage, bare lamps.

In contemporary chandeliers with clear

Match lamp shape...

...with fixture shape.

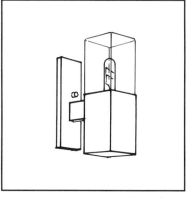

Robert Long

glass chimneys, a tubular-shape lamp elongates the light source and is attractive. In chandeliers that are copies of gas fixtures, a tubular lamp covered with a cloth mantle imitates a gas flame. The chimney lamp (GT) combines a bulb with a chimney, thereby eliminating the necessity of purchasing both. They do not fool anyone, however. The A lamp must be used only in chandeliers designed to hide the lamp, such as chandeliers with shades, opal globes, or frosted chimneys. Never allow an A lamp to be seen.

Most lamps are manufactured in either a candelabra (small) or medium base (standard size) to fit the socket of any chandelier. Adapters can modify a medium-base socket to accept a candelabra size. Be cautious; sometimes the proportions look awkward. Check out an adapter and a lamp in the fixture first, unless the lamps are unseen.

Some lamps will not work in an upside down or horizontal position. Ask the supplier before buying or check the manufacturer's lamp catalog (a useful reference). Match fixture shape with lamp shape.

When lamping a fixture with a clear glass shade, match the lamp shape with the fixture shape. Use a globe lamp in a clear-glass globe shade; use a linear lamp in a linear shade.

The glass in lamps can be clear or coated. Clear glass permits seeing the filament. Coated glass diffuses the filament. Some clear lamps have a tint—iridescent, amber, ruby, smoke, blue, and green. The tint adds a slight hue to the light. Coated lamps are red, orange, and so on, but white is the most common. Frosted lamps are not quite the same as coated; they have a hot spot, because they do not diffuse as well as inside-coated lamps. (The new energy-saving A lamps in higher wattages are coated, but the coating is semitransparent. Treat them as though they were coated lamps; do not substitute them for clear lamps.)

Rule of Thumb for Choosing a Clear or a Coated Lamp

When the lamp can be seen, choose a clear lamp. When the lamp cannot be seen, choose a coated lamp.

This rule sounds backwards, but it is not. Fixtures with clear glass and no shades are designed to show off the lighted filament and look like a candle. Consequently, if the filament is obscured by a coating, the aesthetics are destroyed. Clear glass lamps should give only as much light as a candle. Do not create glare by using more than 15 watts in a clear lamp.

If the manufacturer indicates that a downlight in a decorative fixture (chandelier or pendant) is rated for both A and R lamps, choose an R lamp and lower the wattage. A lower wattage R lamp will produce as much light as a higher wattage A lamp, but it will consume less electricity. However, the fixture must have a porcelain or ceramic socket; brass sockets get too hot for R lamps.

ADVANTAGES/DISADVANTAGES OF LINE VOLTAGE

Line-voltage incandescent can be easily and inexpensively dimmed. Line-voltage lamps are readily available. Turning incandescent sources on and off repeatedly does not harm them.

Advantages/Disadvantages of Line-Voltage Incandescent

Advantages
- inexpensive
- easy to dim
- replacements readily available
- beams easy to control
- mostly point sources
- variety of beam widths
- some linear sources
- turning on/off does not harm
- produces shadows
- creates sparkle and highlights
- good for accent lighting
- good for visible sources

Disadvantages
- produces heat
- consumes more energy
- burns out quickly
- shadows can disadvantage faces
- not good for general distribution

Line-voltage incandescent has several disadvantages. They are not energy efficient. To light something, they require more wattage than fluorescent and more than low voltage properly positioned. Also, they produce heat. In air-conditioned environments, the heat must be removed causing double expenditure of energy to keep the space comfortable. They burn out quickly. Initially, line-voltage incandescent are the least expensive to buy, but ultimately, the most expensive to maintain.

When positioned above the head, they produce unflattering shadows, creating dark recesses at the eyes and a mustache under the nose. Line-voltage incandescent should only be used when no other type of lamp can provide the distribution and intensity desired. Do not use them only because they are familiar and have been used in the past. Many other choices are available.

Lamp technology is producing newer and better sources yearly. Compare the amount of light produced by the lamp, the lamp life, and the beam width to determine which lamp would suit the project.

Low Voltage

Low-voltage incandescent are usually 12 volts, but can be 6, 24, or any voltage that the lamp requires. A transformer reduces the 120 volts to the suitable voltage. At a higher voltage, the lamp will burn out immediately. (I knew that fact. But after carefully carrying a special 12-volt lamp around New York City and on the airplane home, I eagerly hooked it up to a wall receptacle with my alligator clips, cord, and plug. BOOM! I never got to see the beam distribution. I had to reorder. Short incidents can teach long lessons.)

Match the transformer capacity to the wattage needed for the lamps plus 20 percent for a safety margin. Transformers are rated with a volt times amp (VA) rating. Volts multiplied by amps equals watts. (See *Electrical Service* in Chapter 6.)

Transformers are small. Sometimes they are built into the fixture or the track; sometimes they are remotely mounted. All transformers consume electricity—up to 5 percent of the total energy required for the lamps.

Low voltage last longer than line voltage. They are rated at 2,000 to 3,500 hours. The wiring for low-voltage incandescent is the best for remodeling. It can be strung almost anywhere, making installation easy. The required transformer can be mounted remotely, as long as it is accessible and in a well-ventilated location. However, the electricity drops as it travels along the wire, due to distance and wire size. The electricity drop affects the brightness and the color-rendering capabilities of the lamp. Keep voltage drop to 5 percent. Remote transformers with several sources should be centrally located, thereby reducing the distance traveled to each source.

Lamps for low voltage are point sources.

PAR   MR   G   S   B   T   T

Sylvania and Tivoli

Shapes of low-voltage lamps vary. They can be small bubbles of glass (T) for lamp holders, tubes, tapes, or panels; small lamps (S) on strings (wires); multifaceted reflector (MR); car headlight type (PAR); or glass globes (G). Low-voltage tube, tape, or string lights are often called linear by their manufacturers, but they are indeed point sources. They are T or S lamps. The fixtures—tubes, tapes, or strings—are linear; hence referred to as linear lighting.

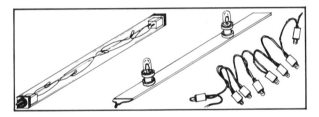

Low-voltage tube, tape, and string.

Some T lamps are double ended; some are single ended. One bipin type in 10 or 20 watts is used in a low-profile fixture (referred to as a hockey puck) to recess into upper cabinets. Since a halogen lamp is used, the fixture should have a glass lens. Halogen lamps can shatter. A lens protects the user.

The engineering of the low-voltage MR and PAR point sources is so good that they have the greatest beam control—very narrow spot, narrow spot, medium flood, flood, and very wide flood. Check exact beam spread in manufacturers' technical data.

G lamps are marvelous glass globes available in a delicate low wattage (2½) for big effects and no glare.

Low-voltage lamp wattages ranges from ¼ to 100 watts—many choices for many different purposes. Lamps in tubes and panels are 2½ watts or less. Most tubes and all panels are sealed and have to be taken down and

sent back to the factory when lamps burn out. However, some tubes open to replace lamps. The replaceable lamp tubes are the best.

Tape lamps are 2 or more watts. Tape lamps are replaceable when they burn out. String lamps are replaceable and can be higher wattage.

Advantages/Disadvantages of Low-Voltage Incandescent

Advantages
- easy wiring for remodeling
- many shapes and forms
- tube, tape, and string have easy installation
- tube, tape, and string are good for visible sources
- small fixtures for MR and T
- transformer easy to hide
- creates sparkle and highlights
- creates shadows
- good for accent lighting
- a whiter-appearing light
- can conserve energy
- higher wattage does not always mean larger lamp
- many beam widths
- many intensities

Disadvantages
- more expensive than line-voltage lamps
- replacements not readily available
- continuous dimming darkens lamp
- not good for general distribution
- expensive to dim
- MR not good for high-ceiling mount
- open MR lamps can shatter
- sealed tubes need replacing when lamps burn out

There are several disadvantages of low voltage lamps. They are more expensive. Many distributors do not carry them and they must be ordered. They can be dimmed, but the transformer and dimming system must be compatible. Continuous dimming may darken the lamp. They must be burned at full brightness to clear the lamp. If the light distribution and intensity is suitable and within budget, use low voltage at lower wattage in preference to line voltage any time.

When comparing low voltage to line voltage, do not jump to the conclusion that the line-voltage higher wattage yields more light. Finely engineered low-voltage sources can yield bright light—as much as 20 percent more. Choose the source according to the amount and spread of light desired.

fluorescent

Fluorescent lamps are line voltage. Contrary to popular belief, fluorescent lamps have the greatest range of light color, unlike incandescent which has a narrow range. Fluorescent can imitate sunlight, north skylight, incandescent, and other colors of light. The cool-white, bluish light used in offices is not the only fluorescent color, but bluish-white is the best for distinguishing black print on new white, not recycled, paper.

Fluorescent lamps require a ballast to synchronize the lamp. The ballast limits the electricity to the range acceptable by the lamp, as determined by the manufacturer. Without this electrical restraint, the lamp would burn out. Therefore, fluorescent lamps must match ballasts in order to operate.

Fluorescent lamps are classified by their starting characteristics, either needing or not needing a starter. Starters are needed by preheat lamps. (A switch initiates heat for preheat lamp starting.) Starters are not needed by instant-start and rapid-start lamps. Rapid-start lamps are the most widely used. They are the <u>only</u> ones that can be dimmed. Instant-start lamps can be distinguished by single-pin ends.

Ballasts are often classified by the lamp-starting characteristics also. Two types of fluorescent ballasts are made. They are magnetic (core-and-coil or reactance) and electronic (solid state). The core-and-coil ballasts are used for rapid-start and for instant-start lamps. Reactance ballasts are used for low-wattage, preheated fluorescent sources, but require an external starter. Ballast type must be compatible with lamp type.

The electronic ballast is also called solid state. They increase source efficacy and eliminate the fluorescent flicker that bothers some people. (See *Ballasts* in Chapter 6.)

Lamps for Fluorescent

Fluorescent lamps are either linear or compact. Linear are subminiature, mini-bipin, or

FLUORESCENT LAMPS

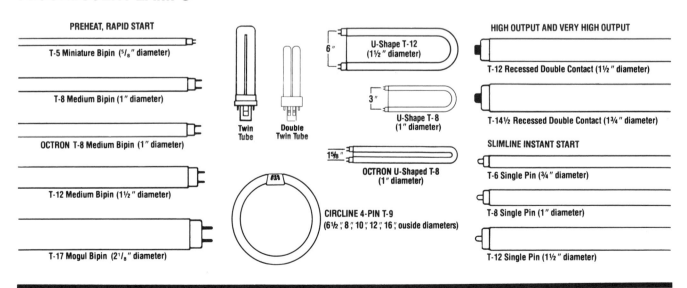

medium-bipin types. Their wattage is tied to their length. Typically, in the medium bipin (T12, 1½ inches in diameter), the 2-foot length is 20 watts, the 3 foot is 30 watts, and the 4 foot is 40 watts. For built-in light fixtures, choose all the same color for consistency and all the same length, if possible, for easy maintenance.

Great changes have occurred in fluorescent lamp sizes. The standard linear in 2-, 3-, or 4-foot lengths have been made thinner, 1-inch diameter (T8). Further, a subminiature is made as thin as your pencil. The subminiature is about ¼ inch in diameter. The 8-inch length is 6 watts, the 12 inch is 8 watts, the 16 inch is 10 watts, and the 20 inch is 13 watts. In addition, linear lamps have been bent to be compact. Compact sizes range from 4 to over 24 inches. The wattages vary from 7 to 39. Compacts have single-bent or double-bent tubes in closed or open bends. Some have plug-in bases. Some are encased in glass with built-in ballasts and screw bases. Some glass enclosures have a reflector, like a PAR lamp. Reflector types are available in 11- and 15-watts and perform like 50- and 75-watt reflector incandescent lamps. The 18- to 27-watt compacts are good for 1-by-1-foot fluorescent troffers. The 39-watt size fits 2-by-2-foot troffers. The long and thin T4 (usually 18 and 26 watts) is suitable for higher ceilings when higher levels of light are required. The short and fat T5 (usually 22 and 28 watts) is good for retrofitting, but anticipate that the light output will be less. The four-tube compacts put out the amount of light that 40- to 100-incandescent watts put out.

The color of light from a compact is similar to incandescent and mixes well. Bases vary. Bases, watts, and ballast requirements must be matched. Do not mix. Overall, compact fluorescent sources offer many energy-efficient options and create pleasing light.

Color of Fluorescent Light

Great changes have occurred in colors of fluorescent light. Typically, the choice has been cool or warm white, with deluxe versions. But color has improved. Now, fluorescent color is anything from cool, somewhat bluish, with cool white (CW) to warm prime colors or triphosphor (30°K). The prime color or triphosphor lamps are called Designer, Ultralume, or SP, depending upon the manufacturer. They are designated by Kelvin color temperature 30° (warm), 35°, or 41° (cool). Kelvin temperatures indicate how warm (reddish) or how cool (bluish) the light appears. The higher the Kelvin number, the bluer the light; the lower the number, the redder the light. A good device for remembering is to think about the sky at sunset. Low on the horizon the sky is red; so remember that low Kelvin temperature is red. The sky high above is blue; so remember that high Kelvin temperature is blue. Higher temperatures of 75° are like overcast skylight. Industry uses 50° to match colors. (Incandescent color at 28° can not do the job.)

Fluorescent light can match the color temperature of incandescent while providing energy efficiency. Compact lamps are lower in temperature (27°) than some incandescent sources.

Advantages/Disadvantages of Fluorescent

Fluorescent lamps last a long time—usually four years in a residence. They are energy efficient. They create very little heat. Both linear and compact produce around 40 percent more light than incandescent. Both last up to 13 times longer. If they are linear, they spread the light. If they are compact, the fixture must spread the light. Both can be built-in architecturally and be unseen light sources. Fluorescent lamps are

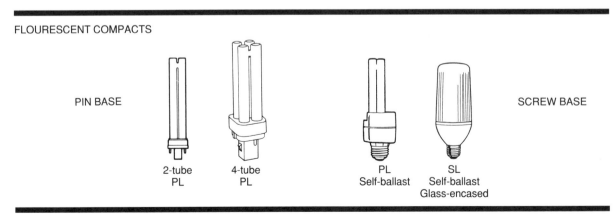

FLOURESCENT COMPACTS

PIN BASE

2-tube PL

4-tube PL

PL Self-ballast

SL Self-ballast Glass-encased

SCREW BASE

disadvantaged by turning on and off repeatedly. (Switching reduces the phosphors inside the lamp, which are required to produce light.) They initially cost more than line-voltage incandescent, but they pay back quickly in reduced energy consumption and fewer lamp replacements. Over time they are less expensive.

Advantages/Disadvantages of Flourescent

Advantages
- burns cool
- lamps last a long time
- energy efficient
- linear light
- minimal shadows
- good for large surface lighting
- some have minimal ultraviolet light that fades colors

Disadvantages
- requires special dimmers
- turning off/on harms lamps
- cost more than line-voltage incandescent
- all range of colors not readily accessible
- does not show texture
- not good for visible sources
- wattage tied to lamp length

Cold Cathode

Cold cathode is a cold version of fluorescent, which is hot cathode. Cold cathode can be custom made in linear or curves, contoured to conform with the architecture. Likewise, it comes in ready-made, linear lengths. Cold cathode produces less light than fluorescent. White cold cathode produces only 420 lumens per foot and white fluorescent produces 750. Many ready-made colors are available, including subtle shades (pink, tangerine, peach, rose, and red, for example). Any custom color can be made, even matching ready-made fluorescent. Cold cathode can be surface mounted or hidden. It is used in coves in soft colors that are not available in fluorescent. It can illuminate the reveal of an arched doorway. Cold cathode requires a transformer to increase the current to the lamp. One transformer can supply 120 feet of lamp. Snap-on reflectors are available to redirect the light where needed. Unlike fluorescent, cold cathode can be dimmed with uniformity and no flickering at the ends. The lamps last 20,000 hours and consume only 10 watts per foot. Cold cathode is an underused decorative light source with great architectural adaptability.

Cold cathode.

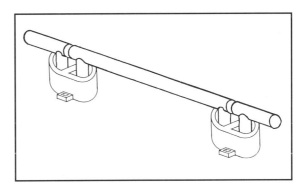

neon

Neon is old technology. It is unexcelled in attention getting and ability to be molded into any shape. However, it cannot provide task lighting. It puts out around 220 lumens per foot, depending upon the color. Like cold cathode, neon is always linear tubes. The tubes are filled with gas. The gas creates the color in a clear tube or the gas in combination with a tinted tube creates the color. Like cold cathode, the tubes can be fashioned in any shape. Neon also requires a transformer to increase the current to the lamp. The transformer must be accessible and in a well-ventilated place. Neon consumes a mere 8 watts per foot. Neon is always custom made. It can be surface mounted or hidden, and is useful for accenting interior architectural features. It has gained popularity in residential spaces as artful sculpture, illuminated handrails and coves, or luminous walls. Surface mounted, they can be visually overpowering and too functional looking. Also, the transformer can be noisy. Skill is required to use neon successfully.

high intensity and laser

High-intensity lamps are sodium, mercury, and metal-halide. Low-wattage, white-sodium lamps could be used in kitchens in the future. Their only drawbacks are instability of color rendering and the need to cool down 10 minutes before relighting. When these characteristics are changed, they will be valuable, low-energy point sources. Mercury and metal-halide, on the other hand, are probably never going to be suitable for kitchens and certainly not for baths.

Laser light is produced by oscillations of atoms or molecules, requiring a controller and a projector. A highly concentrated beam of light is produced in one wavelength or color. Fog or smoke are required in order to see the beam. In residences, alcohol and water foggers are used. Some classes of laser light can damage the eyes and skin. A license is required to use it. However, a Class I beam is not considered dangerous. Nonetheless, it is not a task light. It is only decorative and consequently will probably never be used for kitchens or baths.

HIGH INTENSITY DISCHARGE LAMPS

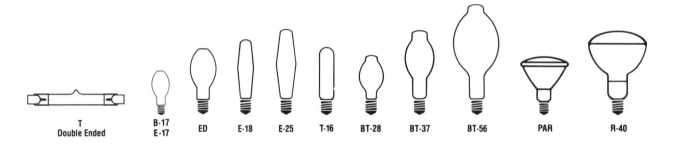

T
Double Ended   B-17
E-17   ED   E-18   E-25   T-16   BT-28   BT-37   BT-56   PAR   R-40

Sylvania

how to choose

Lamp manufacturers indicate first what the wattage of a lamp is. Then, they designate lamps by a letter code indicating the shape and numbers indicating the largest diameter in eighths of an inch. Consequently, an incandescent F15 lamp is flame shaped and fifteen-eights in diameter or $1\frac{7}{8}$ inches, and a fluorescent T12 is tubular shaped and twelve-eights in diameter or $1\frac{1}{2}$ inches. A designation of 100A19 is read as a 100 watt A lamp that is $2\frac{3}{8}$ inches in diameter.

In addition, manufacturers identify lamps by a description of their bases. Screw-base lamps for decorative fixtures are either medium or candelabra size to fit medium- or candelabra-size sockets. One does not fit the other. Bases for recessed fixtures vary greatly. Most are screw bases; some are bipins, bayonets, or terminals requiring screws. These distinctions help identify the lamp.

Finally, manufacturers indicate the voltage, 120, 12, 6, etc., so that lamp choices will be compatible with fixture choices.

Lamps should be chosen before fixtures. Choose lamps for their intensity and distribution that makes the lighting design work. Lamps deliver intensity and create the distribution. The fixture holds the lamp in place and aims it. Consequently, choose lamps, not fixtures, early in the design process. Poor quality fixtures or improperly positioned lamps can destroy available intensity and distribution.

Distances from lamps to the surface lighted and the angle of the light are critical to determining the intensity of the light. Use the quick-calculation data from fixture manufacturers. This data permits rudimentary choices for determining intensities and beam widths. Hand or computer calculations can refine choices.

In general, for kitchen countertop tasks, choose fluorescent whenever possible. For kitchen eating surfaces and sinks in states that do not restrict the use of incandescent sources in kitchens, choose incandescent point sources, either line or low voltage. For general kitchen lighting, choose fluorescent. For nontask kitchen surfaces, choose low voltage.

For bath mirrors and reading tasks, choose fluorescent. For tubs and showers, choose compact fluorescent or incandescent for tasks. For nontask surfaces, choose low-voltage incandescent.

In general, narrow beams of light come from spot lamps, either PAR, MR, or R. Wide beams come from A, PAR, MR, or R floods.

All the energy-saving sources, such as 65-, 90-, or 120-watt PAR or the 67- or 90-watt A, reduce energy consumption but also deliver less lumens (the unit of light coming from the source). The reduction is anywhere from 60 to 320 lumens. However, it is considered barely noticeable for many situations. Choose the most energy-efficient lamp that can do the job, regardless of cost. Energy-saving sources will pay back the initial cost and continue saving.

Each type of lamp renders colors differently. Color rendering is a crucial measure of lighting quality. A color-rendering index of 100 indicates that colors appear true to life—what we expect colors to look like under daylight or incandescent lamps. Lower indexes indicate that colors would appear distorted. But we do not always see the distortion. Our memory of color takes over and recalls that the tomato is red, not muddy red. High indexes mean that food would look more appealing in the kitchen, and faces made up at the bathroom mirror would look natural in the daylight.

How well a lamp renders colors and how energy efficient it is are usually mutually exclusive. For example, incandescent that has a high color-rendering index is low in energy efficiency. However, the newer fluorescent linear and compact lamps have good color-rendering indexes and are also high in energy efficiency. Choose lamps for kitchens and baths that have high color-rendering abilities as well as high energy efficiency.

Compare indexes only if lamps have a Kelvin temperature within 300 degrees of each other. Kelvin temperature and color-rendering indexes must be used in conjunction with each other and used cautiously. They are not absolutes.

When mixing nonhalogen incandescent and linear fluorescent sources within a kitchen or bath, choose fluorescent sources with low Kelvin temperature—the warm whites or 30°K lamps. Compact fluorescent sources are made with low Kelvin temperatures and do not offer choices. Incandescent light is around 28°K. When mixing halogen with linear fluorescent sources, choose 35°K. Fluorescent can blend well with any incandescent.

Use clear lamps whenever lamps are seen.

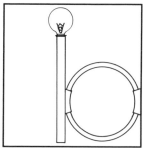

Use coated lamps whenever lamps cannot be seen.

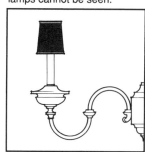

When choosing decorative fixtures, incandescent lamps are necessary. Line-voltage decorative lamps can mix or match the fixture style. They can be clear or coated. Use clear lamps in low wattage whenever the lamps will be seen. Use coated lamps whenever the lamps will not be seen (lamps behind shades).

When choosing recessed or track fixtures, fluorescent, low-voltage, or low-wattage line-voltage incandescent are good. Fit the lamp's performance capability to the job and pick the most energy-efficient lamp to do it. Fluorescent is the most energy efficient and low-voltage spots are the most brilliant. The wide range of lamps gives the designer choices for creative intents.

Choose the lamp that can perform the way you want it. Then, find the fixture that can hold it. Sometimes, redesign is required, if constraints make the lamp of choice impossible. The final choice is a merger of considerations: aesthetics, electrical service, structural constraints, cost, design intent, and client's needs. For instance, owners are more likely to invest more dollars in the lighting and their lighting can be built-in. Renters, however, are confined to portable fixtures that can travel with them. Both can have good light from great light sources.

chapter 5

fixtures

Fixtures can be classified by whether they are visible or not so visible. Not-so-visible fixtures are either recessed or built-in, becoming an integral part of the structure. Visible fixtures are in view and can be lighting jewelry for kitchens and baths.

not so visible

Places for Not-So-Visible Fixtures in Kitchen and Baths

- under base cabinets in toe spaces
- in a bracket over the sink
- in a canopy over an island
- in the ceiling
- under ceramic tile overhangs
- in a cornice over mural wallpaper
- in a cove above upper cabinets
- in a dropped soffit
- in glass block walls
- in handrails
- under the platform of a raised tub
- in the backsplash as a luminous panel
- in the overhang of stair treads
- inside coffers at wall/ceiling edges
- under upper cabinets
- in a valance over a window
- at any of the other ingenious places to put task or nontask lighting

The places for not-so-visible fixtures are limited only by one's imagination and the client's financial resources.

Not-so-visible fixtures can be divided into two groups: purchasable ready-made fixtures or custom-made fixtures, usually built-in.

Ready-Made Recessed Fixtures

- accent lights
- downlights
- framing projectors
- perimeter troffers or concealed track system
- wall washers
- heat lights

Ready-Made Recessed Fixtures

Recessed fixtures are excellent for putting light onto a surface from a minimally seen source.

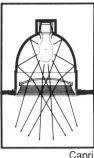

Well-engineered recessed fixture.

Capri

Recessed fixtures can create many settings for kitchens and baths that are not obtainable by any other type of lighting, because they are essentially out of sight. Recessed fixtures can hold a heat source to warm up a bathroom, rather than warming up a whole house. Recessed fixtures can create sparkle, carve out, expand, or punctuate a space. They can provide a lot of or a little light that harmonizes or contrasts. With open recessed fixtures, the ceiling is not bright; surfaces—countertops, tabletops, walls, furniture, and floors—are bright. Consequently, surfaces attract attention.

Some recessed fixtures are well engineered. Choose them to get the most light for the money and the least fixture recognition. Some recessed fixtures put light straight down (downlights). Some put it to the side (wall washers, accent lights, framing projectors, and perimeter troffers). How the incandescent fixture looks does not always indicate the distribution it produces. Do not try to guess what it does. Read the manufacturer's technical data.

Never put a recessed fixture above a ceiling paddle fan. The lighting effect is flick, flick, flick—very irritating, particularly when trying to do a task.

Skillfully placed, well-engineered lighting equipment can create settings in theaters. In commercial spaces, settings are created by recessed fixtures to highlight products. Likewise, settings can be created in kitchens and baths to emphasize, soothe, or brighten. What kind of setting do you want?

Adjustable accent.

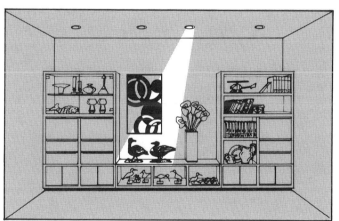

Framing projector.

Wall washing.

Downlight/wall washing.

Create a brilliantly sparkling counter- or table-top with light. It is attention getting and cheerful. Colors and objects become vivid and appealing. Contrast the setting to a dim background. Make the surface bright. The setting draws people to it. The closer the light is confined to the tabletop, the more intimate the impression.

Sprinkle a horizontal surface with sparkle.

A ceiling-recessed downlight, downlight in a chandelier, or framing projector can provide this kind of setting. MR, PAR, or R lamps will do it best. In most residences, energy-saving, low-voltage MR16 50-watt medium to wide beam or PAR 35- or 50-watt spot or flood will do the trick. Otherwise, a line-voltage 65-watt, a 75-watt PAR flood from the ceiling, or a 50-watt reflector from a chandelier will be sufficient. For more brilliance, add more wattage. For narrow beams of light, use spots.

Match the beam spread to the dimensions of the top. For a perfect match, use a framing projector or a track fixture with barn doors to confine the beam.

Sample Electric Cost

The electrical cost for one fixture with a 50-watt lamp at 10¢ per kilowatt-hour for 4 hours per night for a year would be $7.20, about equal to one night at the movies with a soft drink and popcorn.

CARVE OUT A SPACE WITHIN A SPACE

A space can be defined by downlights. The light need not be brilliant, but surrounding light must be dimmer in order not to loose the effect of the carved-out space. For example, downlight, focused on a kitchen eating area inviting you to join in, visually organizes the seating area with consistent light. Light creates seemingly three-dimensional but penetrable walls. It is soothing and yet sociable. The illuminated area seems to be alone and suggests you sit back and enjoy the meal.

For a softly illuminated area in residences, use low-voltage, 50-watt flood lamps, PAR or MR16. For a vividly illuminated area,

Carve out a space within a space.

use line-voltage 65- to 90-watt PARs. Position the downlights over the center of the table, never over the chairs. (Downlight would produce ghoulish shadows on the faces of the people seated.)

Sample Electric Cost

The electrical cost for one 50-watt and three 30-watt downlights for 4 hours per night for a month at 10¢ per kilowatt-hour would be $1.68, a little more than the cost of a Sunday newspaper.

A softly illuminated seating area of one small sofa, two chairs, and a coffee table in a kitchen-family room would require three downlights, either 30-watt line voltage or 20-watt low voltage. Position the fixtures over the front edge of the cushions of the two chairs and over the middle of the coffee table (not glass, however) to fill the interior of the area.

Rule of Thumb for Glass-Top Table

Never use recessed downlights, open or covered, over a glass-top table. The glare never goes away.

EXPAND A SPACE WITH WIDESPREAD LIGHT

An area of a kitchen or bath can be expanded by light, exploding the space and fostering an atmosphere that encourages people to move around freely. Light reveals the richness of the area. It is stimulating. To light uniformly, use either ceiling-recessed fixtures or many light sources at different locations spreading the light evenly. If recessed downlights are chosen, the amount of light from each fixture should be the same, and the fixtures should be spaced evenly. When choosing a fixture, consider personal preference about the fixture's aesthetics and coordinate light-delivery capabilities. Wide-beam downlights can do the job, but fluorescent fixtures will produce a more uniform illumination. Fluorescent is recommended because it conserves energy. Either way, make sure no distracting brightness is seen. Use an opal diffuser in kitchens or baths rather than a prismatic lens. Parabolic louvers avoid ceiling brightness and put light down on countertops or other table-height surfaces. However, parabolic louvers do not light faces will in baths.

Widespread light.

When using incandescent downlights to expand a space, create uniform light by positioning the fixtures evenly spaced. The distance between fixtures can be determined with the spacing criteria. Downlight manufacturers indicate spacing criteria in their technical catalogs. They are the maximum distances their fixtures can be apart and still deliver uniform light. (The criteria does not indicate how bright the uniform light will be.) The spacing criterion multiplied by the height above the surface to be lighted (usually the floor, possibly a tabletop) equals the space between fixtures. The space between a fixture and the wall should be half the distance between the fixtures.

Rule of Thumb for Spacing Fixtures

Spacing = spacing criterion x height above the surface to be lighted

Spacing criteria for downlights range from 0.3 to 1.4. The greater the criterion, the farther apart the fixtures can be installed. For example, in a room with 8-foot ceilings, fixtures with a spacing criterion of 1 should be centered 8 feet apart; fixtures with a criterion of 1.4 should be centered 11 feet 2 inches apart. Often, actual installation distance must be modified, because room sizes cannot always be divided evenly by spacing criteria. When modifying, be aware that the closer a fixture is to a wall, the more likely a scallop of light will be formed on that wall. Sometimes the scallop does not conform to the architectural details. Scallops off center or half on and half off visually disturb an interior setting. Determine any disadvantages in the planning stage, not after installation.

If a specific footcandle level must be delivered, spacing criteria might not work and more complicated calculations will have to be made. If fixtures are too far apart, the light becomes scattered, chopping up the space rather than unifying it. If spaced correctly, the light is uniform.

PUNCTUATE A DISTINCTIVE SMALL AREA WITH SATINY LIGHT

A small bay window in a kitchen can be illuminated and be energy efficient. From the outside, the lighted bay window greets and says goodbye. When the room is lighted and full of people, the downlight balances the other illumination. The downlight need not

A lighted bay window as a nightlight.

be bright. If the surrounding light is not overpowering, a 20-watt MR16 flood or a 30-watt R can be bright enough. If the surrounding light is bright, 50 or 75 watts may be necessary.

Likewise, a tub alcove with windows can be illuminated efficiently in the same way. Such a light can be a nightlight, giving a reassuring glimmer.

Sample Electric Cost

Only 36¢ worth of electricity is used for a 30-watt downlight operating 4 hours per night for a whole month at 10¢ per kilowatt-hour, less than the cost of a crisp apple.

Many other settings can be formed with downlights. Determine what is to be emphasized and how vivid it should be. Of course, the more vivid it is, the more attention it will draw. But not all settings require brightness or should be bright. Remember, vivid light is stimulating; soft light is soothing. Decide which mood you want.

In addition, the mood can be changed with a dimmer, but colors might also change. On the one hand, as incandescent light dims,

Make sure scallops of light conform to the architecture.

it turns more golden, like the inside of a pumpkin. It gives the appearance of being warmer, enhancing red colors in the space, but it makes other colors appear muddy. On the other hand, fluorescent does not change color but is more costly to dim.

Settings can be created by downlight.

Wilsonart

UNDERLINE WALL TEXTURE WITH GRAZING

Grazing is created by aiming light at a shallow angle to a vertical textured surface. The light enhances horizontal texture or other surface qualities, all of which should be intended. If the surface has unintended flaws, the light calls attention to them and they become predominant. Do not graze plaster or drywall that is only painted. Graze a wall covered with textured wallpaper, fabric, or masonry, particularly where the mortar has been removed from the edges (raked joints). A masonry wall and textured cabinets stand up and sing with grazing light.

Requirements for Grazing Light

- Position fixtures 6 to 8 inches out from the surface.
- Use incandescent reflector lamps. A lamps do not concentrate the light enough, and fluorescent is too shadow free.
- Conceal lamps well, especially from view when seated.
- Place fixtures close together.
- Keep fixtures out of sight and unimposing, either as recessed fixtures or track fixtures behind a cornice board.
- Use a well-engineered fixture and reflector lamp (R or PAR) to produce the greatest amount of light with the least electricity.

Recessed Fixtures

Owners who are building and relighting can use recessed fixtures for dramatic wall grazing. Recessed fixtures focus all the attention on the wall. Make sure that the fixture chosen does not create any flashback of light from the edge of the rim. Not all fixtures are well designed. Some even show an image of the lamp on the reflector. Choose one that does not. Inspect recessed fixtures in your local showroom.

The greater the wattage of the lamp, the more intense the shadows. However, good shadows come from 50-watt R lamps, if fixtures are well designed and if the surface color is not too dark. If dark, a 75-watt or higher lamp is necessary. Determine the color of the wall before buying fixtures. Dark walls (and higher ceilings) require more lamp wattage than pale walls (and standard ceilings). Dark walls are rich looking and attractive but they require more light.

Install the fixtures 6 to 8 inches out and 12 to 16 inches apart, evenly spaced. The further the spread, the deeper the scallops. Distance at the ends should be half the distance between fixtures. Uneven spacing will be apparent, creating uneven scallops and uneven light. The wall will be brighter at the top and softly lighted down the wall, depending upon the wattage chosen. For example, the effect of using the 75-watt spot is a strong stroke of light touching the wall all the way down. It puts out enough light to glance at a cookbook or find shoes easily but not enough to read the small print on a pill bottle.

The system can be dimmed. Often, dimmers have been used where the initial wattage was too much for the space and the brightness had to be cut down to what it should have been in the first place. This practice is poor lighting design. Instead, dim to extend the life of the lamps, especially if the installation is not in a convenient location to change lamps. But in addition, dimming changes the color temperature of light and emphasizes the red end of the spectrum. Therefore, dimmed light could be used to enhance, for example, red tones on a brick wall. Other colors might be disadvantaged by dimming.

When building, plan for sufficient ceiling depth for wall-grazing fixtures. When remodeling, the depth must be available and wiring must be gained through an attic or pulled from elsewhere. If ceiling wiring is not obtainable, owners will have to use the portable or surface-mounted wall-grazing fixtures.

Graze a textured wall.

Track Fixtures

Renters do not have the options that owners have to recess fixtures. Nonetheless, renters can have dramatic grazing light by two means:

either track fixtures surface mounted on the ceiling and hooked up with a cord and plug, or bare lamps with lamp holders behind a cornice board. Surface-mounted track fixtures have their own shielding and can be installed along the wall, pointing almost straight down. Bare lamps on a track need a cornice board to shield them from view.

Sample Electric Cost

Light for an 8-foot wall using six fixtures of 50 watts each for 4 hours per night at 10¢ per kilowatt-hour costs $3.60 per month. The amount is no more than would be required for two table lamps, and yet two table lamps could not light a whole wall.

To make a cornice board, follow the directions in *Cornices* in this chapter. However, mount the board at least 8 inches and up to 12 inches away from the wall, depending upon the wattage of the lamp (higher wattage lamps are bigger). Lamps of 75 watts or less require cornice boards to be 8 inches from the wall; 150-watt lamps require cornice boards to be 12 inches from the wall. When ceilings are 9 feet or less, suitable installation is 8 inches out, and suitable wattage is 75 or less.

Make the board 12½ inches deep with a 3-inch return or less at the bottom. The track should be mounted on the inside of the board. The outside of the board can be trimmed, painted, or otherwise finished to fit and coordinate with the wall. Install a cornice board as long as the wall to be grazed and adjust the track fixture to point down.

Use the simplest track fixture—a lamp holder—and equip it with a spot lamp. These fixtures are functional-looking and must be hidden.

The precise alignment and wattage need not be determined before installation. Changes of spacing and wattage can be made after.

Owners can install a recessed, concealed track system along the wall. These slick, engineered fixtures give optimal light with minimal aperture (2 inches). They use MR16 low-voltage lamps. Housings are available in several lengths that can be continuous. In addition, for nontextured wall coverings, recessed fluorescent troffers can also be continuous perimeter lighting. Perimeter lighting is good for exercise areas with a mirrored wall in bathrooms. It lights the mirror and avoids direct glare for the exerciser who must, at times, lie on his/her back.

Sample Electric Cost

A cornice system using eight 50-watt fixtures recessed along an 8-foot wall and used for 4 hours at 10¢ per kilowatt-hour costs $4.80 per month.

A built-in system for the same wall equipped with 75-watt spots costs $7.20 per month.

Even at the higher wattage, the yearly additional cost of electricity for a wall-grazing system is about the same as four tanks of gas for the family car.

BRING A WALL INTO FOCUS WITH WALL WASHING

Walls with special coverings, murals, wall paper, or paneling can be illuminated to reveal colors and bring them into view. A well-engineered, recessed, wall-washing, fluorescent system is available. It has an excellent reflector and offset lamp arrangement that positions one lamp below the ceiling line, protected from view and giving an even wash of light from 2 feet back from the wall. Two fluorescent lamps are used and fixtures are available from 2 to 8 feet long with vertical louvers.

Bring a wall into focus with wall washing.

Likewise, a wall-washing incandescent system can be used, but it consumes more electricity and puts out heat. Manufacturers recommend fixture placement based on distance back from the wall and desired brightness for average room-surface reflectance. Compare the reflectance values with the ones the manufacturers are assuming. Calculations might be needed to gain the desired effect. If A lamps are to be used, use at least three to light a wall; fewer fixtures do not give an even wash.

EFFECTS

The lighting effects for settings range from broad to focused, from harmonizing to contrasting, and from soft to vivid. When the whole room is illuminated, a social, gregarious atmosphere is created. When an intimate space is illuminated and the rest of the space is dim, people are drawn to the lighted area. When the walls are illuminated, a self-contained, soothing atmosphere is created. The effect of downlights depends not only on the engineering of the fixture but also on the type of lamp used. Some downlights are engineered with reflectors to concentrate the light; others spread the light. Fixtures that put light straight down produce wide, medium, or narrow lighted areas. The appearance of the fixture does not always indicate the width of the light it produces. For example, a pinhole looks like it produces a narrow beam of light, but it does not. It produces a medium beam if the lamp is properly adjusted. A narrow beam is produced by an open fixture equipped with a very narrow spot lamp. Do not try to guess the amount of light a downlight produces; consult the manufacturer's catalog, a knowledgeable salesperson, or a lighting consultant.

OPTIC ENGINEERING

Optic-engineering features of a fixture are internal or external. Internal features are reflectors and adjustments. Reflectors, the first internal feature, redirect, spread, or concentrate light from within the fixture. Some reflectors are better designed than others. The best reflectors enhance the light and do not reflect the lamp's image at usual viewing angles (45°). Reflectors are either specular, semispecular, or satin. The finish dictates how the light will be reflected. Specular finishes redirect light in the same, but opposite, angle it hits the reflector. Semispeculars reflect by spreading some light and do not reflect the lamp image when lit. Satin diffuses light in all directions. Different applications require different reflectors.

Reflector showing lamp image.

In general, cone reflectors redirect light, especially from incandescent A and compact fluorescent lamps. Cones are specular, silver (considered clear), gold, or black. The color of the cone affects the amount and color of light. Likewise, black cones show dust, requiring continual maintenance. All cones show fingerprints—usually a problem in commercial spaces but not necessarily in residential. In addition, the color of cones is not consistent among manufacturers.

Ellipsoidal reflectors redirect and focus the light through a small aperture for a medium to broad distribution. They are the only reflectors that can redeliver light from silvered-bowl lamps.

Similarly, parabolic reflectors redirect the light but through a wider aperture. They are best when combined with black baffles to catch the stray light at the aperture.

Before specifying, determine at a distance how much brightness (or flashback) the fixture's reflector creates from the edge of the rim. The optimum choice is, of course, no brightness.

Multifaceted reflectors for low-voltage halogen T lamps redirect the light from the fixture. The fixtures for these lamps are sometimes called a hockey puck because they have such a low profile (¾ of an inch). They can be surface mounted or recessed. However, never use an open halogen fixture; the lamp may

Cone reflector.   Elliptical reflector.   Parabolic reflector.

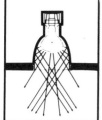 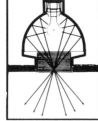 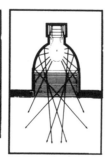

Capri

shatter. Choose a fixture with a lens; it is a necessary safety feature. (Or, choose a MR lamp with a pressed-glass cover.)

The second internal-engineering feature is adjustment. Adjustments permit the light source to be reaimed for accenting or compensating for a sloped ceiling.

Adjustable fixture.

Capri

External features are lenses, diffusers, baffles, and louvers. Lenses cover the opening of the fixture and bend light in some way. A Fresnel lens concentrates light. A spread lens (45° lateral prism) redirects it left and right. A prismatic lens provides uniform, well-diffused lighting, but it can appear bright. To make the best use of a lens, the lamp needs to be the exact wattage specified by the manufacturer. Then, light will be precisely focused. The engineering of a downlight can be ruined by the wrong light source.

Prismatic lens.

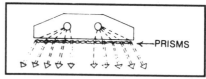
Lightolier

Diffusers also cover the aperture, uniformly obscure the source, and scatter light. One manufacturer makes a high-abuse diffuser for commercial countertop lighting (health care facilities, etc.). Opal diffusers are the best. Usually they are a dropped shape, which puts some light on the ceiling. But when the dropped diffuser is the only light source, they are bright. In some situations they are glaring. Smooth out the brightness with additional sources. An opal diffuser reduces the amount of light. So, consider benefits of uniform diffusion against the disadvantage of

External engineering.

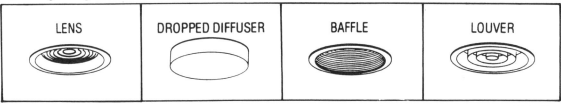

| LENS | DROPPED DIFFUSER | BAFFLE | LOUVER |

Lightolier

Wide.

Medium.

Narrow.

reduced light. (I go for diffusion and add additional fixtures.)

Baffles (black rings in the inner surface of incandescent fixtures or vertical parallel fins in fluorescent fixtures) or louvers (metalwork over the aperture) also reduce aperture brightness. Some louvers are unidirectional, intended to throw light in the direction they are pointed. Some redirect the light down (parabolic or hex-minicell). Utilize these high-quality engineering features to their advantage.

All recessed fixtures can be described in terms of how they distribute light: wide, medium, or narrow; adjustable accent; wall washer; framing projector; or downlight/wall washer.

A wide-beam downlight illuminates a large area. A medium-beam downlight illuminates an area where the activity and objects to be viewed are important—a counter- or tabletop, a seating area, or furniture. (The space becomes more important and activity becomes less important when walls are illuminated.) A narrow-beam downlight highlights special areas or objects. In rooms with high ceilings, many narrow-beam downlights can illuminate a large area because they become wide beams at table-height surfaces. In addition, both wall-washer and adjustable-accent fixtures are engineered to put light to one side. Adjustable-accent fixtures can point to the side or can compensate and shoot light straight down from a sloping ceiling. Some are internally adjustable and others are externally adjustable. Likewise, a framing projector shoots light either straight down or to the side. It produces a sharp-edged light beam. Finally, a downlight/wall washer is very useful for lighting two different surfaces at one time. It permits some light to fall down, as well as some to be directed to one or two walls, or even to a corner.

Some recessed fixtures are not well engineered. They are essentially tin cans with sockets. They can trap light. They have shal-

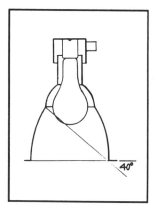

Cutoff angle.

Edison Price

low cutoff angles (the angle up from 0° where the lamp can no longer be seen). Often, more tin cans are required than well-engineered fixtures to do the intended design. In addition, well-engineered fixtures are not necessarily the most expensive in the long run. Fewer are needed to light a space with fewer lamp replacements, using less total wattage. Each manufacturer makes several quality lines, from well engineered to standard. They vary in price. Because of the competition in lighting, some budget-priced fixtures are reasonably engineered and are suitable for many residences and commercial spaces with 8-foot ceilings. High or sloped ceilings definitely require deeper, more expensive fixtures with higher quality light delivery.

The National Electrical Code requires recessed downlights to be either the insulated-ceiling (IC) or the thermal-protected (TP or TC) type. IC can be safely covered with insulation. TP or TC has a protection device but must be installed 3 inches away from insulation, ceiling joists, and other flammable materials.

LAMPS FOR RECESSED FIXTURES

Recessed lighting can be incandescent or fluorescent. Choose fluorescent whenever possible. It uses energy wisely. Linear and compact fluorescent lamps can be housed in not-so-visible fixtures. Some are well hidden from view, like a recessed perimeter coffer; some are more visible, like a fluorescent skylight.

Linear fluorescent fixtures are best for broad distribution of light, whether from the ceiling, under the upper cabinet, or behind leaded glass in a backsplash position. Not-so-visible linear fluorescent fixtures are inexpensive channels. They yield medium- to high-intensity light.

Compact fluorescent fixtures are best for low- to medium-intensity light. As downlights, the fixtures need to be well engineered to take the nonpoint source and redirect the light down. In a vertical position, a compact fluorescent lamp gives a narrow distribution. In a horizontal position, it gives a wider distribution. The only drawback of a compact fluorescent fixture is that sometimes the cone at the aperture reflects a rainbow of color from the compact lamp. Inspect the fixture or question the manufacturer's rep about their solution to this problem. One manufacturer has eliminated this effect in their 13-, 18-, and 26-watt downlights. They are excellent.

Incandescent recessed fixtures can be line or low voltage. Choose low voltage whenever possible in 8-foot ceilings. They can be lower wattage and conserve energy. Choose line voltage whenever the ceilings are higher than 8 feet because they can deliver down to the room-surface levels. Never expect to create general illumination with either type of incandescent fixture. They are point sources and distribute light in a cone. Consequently, too many would be required to light uniformly.

Recessed fixtures accommodate a wide range of sources, from 9 to 300 watts, either incandescent, line- or low-voltage, or compact fluorescent. Many incandescent downlights accept more than one wattage or type of source. These fixtures are internally adjustable to ensure that the source is in the position to deliver the most light. If they are not properly adjusted, light is wasted within the fixture. Many are deep enough for a compact fluorescent with an adaptor, but without a reflector to redirect the fluorescent light, they are not effective.

When choosing between line-voltage A, PAR, or R, there is a trade-off. A lamps produce more light per watt, but emit light on all

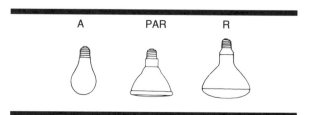

| A | PAR | R |

Lightolier

sides of the lamp, causing some to get trapped in the fixture. They should be used in 10-foot or less ceilings. A lamps are less expensive to buy, but burn out quicker. A lamps come in several versions, A 19, 21, and 23. Choose the A lamp specified for the fixture, because the lamp must fit the fixture properly to provide as much light as possible. Silvered-bowl A lamps require elliptical reflectors to redirect their light. PARs, Rs, and ERs are more expensive than standard A, but last longer. Consider tungsten-halogen PAR. It lasts and is excellent for any fixture that is hard to reach, commercial and residential.

When choosing between low-voltage MR and PAR, the choice is clearly made by what amount of footcandles and beam width are desirable. Consult fixture manufacturers' catalogs, particularly their track catalogs, for lamp beam and intensity information.

A halogen low-voltage lamp (T) with a bipin base is used in retail business. The low-profile fixture holding the lamp is small enough (¾ of an inch thick and called a hockey puck) to recess in upper cabinets or shelves. They are 10 or 20 watts and produce the typical incandescent heat. Use them where bright light is required and heat is not a problem.

Each fixture is manufactured to efficiently use the specified source. All incandescent sources produce heat. Consequently, the line-voltage fixture must have a ceramic socket for Rs and PARs. Follow the manufacturers' specifications for source type and do not try to outwit the engineering of a fixture.

Low-voltage incandescent sources (MR and PAR) are good for 8-foot ceilings. If higher, light is lost and the sources are ineffective.

Different light sources have different requirements for reflectors and other engineering features. A lamps and tubular-halogen lamps need reflectors to do an efficient job. PAR, ER, and R lamps have built-in reflectors, but they need to be deeply recessed to prevent direct glare. The aperture should be baffled or louvered to reduce the glare. MRs also have reflectors built-in, but MRs not encased in glass need a lens to prevent glass from falling if the lamp shatters. (Never handle an MR without gloves or a cloth; oils from fingers can cause the lamp to shatter when lighted.)

Compact fluorescent lamps are suitable for downlighting. They are not point sources. They are linear. Hence, they cannot be focused like incandescent. Consequently, compact fluorescent works best in fixtures designed for them. Downlights use one or two compact lamps in a horizontal or axial position. Compact fluorescent lamps are efficient and long lasting. Wattages range from 7 to 39. Some are dimmable. Sizes vary from 4 to over 22 inches. Some contain ballasts. All compacts are bent-glass tubes but differ in shape and number of tubes (two or four). Some are long and thin; others are short and fat. Some tubes (usually the 9- and 13-watt sizes) are in a globe or in a glass reflector with a built-in ballast. Bases vary. Bases, wattage, and ballast requirements must be matched for each fixture. Fluorescent downlights are excellent for producing low-ambient light and not adding heat to strain air-conditioning.

INSTALLATION

Recessed fixtures are the least conspicuous, and enhance the spontaneous effect of the setting. Recessed fixtures are easy to install in new construction. They can be installed in remodeling wood-frame structures, if an electric junction box is available in the ceiling or the wires can be pulled from an attic or an adjacent space to create one. In new construction or remodeling, the electricity must be controlled by a wall switch. Renters and owners of concrete and steel structures must use surface-mounted, not recessed, downlights.

All recessed fixtures require sufficient space to be put above the finished ceiling. In wooden frame construction, if ceiling joists are not deep (8 or less inches), shallow recessed fixtures are required. However, such fixtures often have the lamp face at the aperture, and it is glaring when lit. Deeper semirecessed (dropped partially below the ceiling) or surface-mounted downlights could be used and avoid the glare. (See *Functional Fixtures* in this chapter.)

Some recessed fixtures have sloped ceiling adapters. Some do not. If not, an adaptable fixture can compensate for the slope.

Some fixtures are semirecessed. A well-engineered, semirecessed wall washer with a halogen lamp is designed to function with one-third to one-half as many fixtures for the same wall as standard wall washers. Further, eyeball trims hang below the ceiling and are semirecessed.

As required by the National Electrical Code, fixture housings are engineered to be covered or not covered with insulation. The insulated-ceiling type (IC) can be covered with insulation. They are suitable for new construction and some remodeling. The thermal-protected type (TP or TC) cannot be covered with insulation and must be 3 inches away from anything. They have an internal switch that turns them off if they get too hot. They are suitable between floors and for most remodeling. An incorrect type could cause a fire!

Before thermal requirements, all recessed fixtures were installed 3 feet away from insulation. Now, insulated-ceiling, recessed fixtures can be covered with insulation and will prevent loss of heat or air-conditioning.

Recessed Fixture Vocabulary

Accent: fixture with adjustable lamp holder.

Adjustable: fixture with lamp holder that reaims the light, vertically or horizontally.

Aperture: fixture's opening at the ceiling.

Baffle: circular or parallel grid over aperture or rings stepped back from aperture.

Ballast: regulating device for fluorescent.

Built-In: housing constructed on site for a fixture to fit the architecture or cabinets.

Channel: linear housing for low voltage or linear lamps, either flourescent or incandescent.

Cone: reflector around the opening of a fixture.

Cutoff Angle: angle up from 0° at which the lamp can no longer be seen.

Diffuser: covering over aperture that uniformly controls light.

Downlight: fixture that puts light down only.

Downlight/Wall Washer: fixture that puts light down and to a wall.

Electric Junction Box: protective container to hook fixture to electrical wires.

Elliptical Reflector: reflector with a curve based on the ellipse.

Fluorescent Skylight: large recessed ceiling-mount fluorescent fixture, flat, sloped, or domed.

Fluorescent Troffer: recessed ceiling-mounted fluorescent fixture.

Framing Projector: fixture with adjustable aperture devices to finely control the light.

Fresnel Lens: a lens that redirects the light to parallel rays.

Housing: recessed portion of fixture with lamp holder and internal engineering features.

Hockey Puck: a low-profile halogen cabinet fixture (not a brand name).

IC: insulated-ceiling recessed fixture.

Lamping and Aiming: installing lamps and adjusting fixtures for best distribution of light.

Lens: aperture covering that alters light delivery.

Louver: grid that shields lamp from view.

Low Profile: fixture for shallow ceiling-joist depths.

Luminaire: fixture with lamp.

Luminous Panel: transparent or translucent materials on surface with fixtures behind.

Opal Diffuser: milky-colored aperture covering, usually in a dropped shape.

Parabolic Louver: louver that redirects light down due to parabolic curves.

Prismatic Lens: lens using nonparallel sides of prisms to redirect light.

Recessed: fixture housing installed behind wall or ceiling surface.

Recessed Perimeter: a coffer at wall/ceiling edge to hold fixtures above the ceiling, usually wall to wall.

Reflector: surface engineered to redirect light in a certain way.

Retrofit: putting new parts (reflector, lamp type, etc.) in a fixture already installed.

Scallop: arch of light falling on wall from a recessed fixture.

Semirecessed: a fixture partially recessed into the ceiling.

Sloped-Ceiling Adaptor: adjustable housing for sloped ceilings.

Spacing Criteria: a number used to calculate recessed fixture placement to create uniform light.

Strip: linear device for low-voltage lamp holders or a fluorescent lamp holder.

Tape: flat wire with low-voltage lamp holders.

Thermal Control (TC): recessed fixture for noninsulated ceilings.

Thermal Protected (TP): recessed fixture for noninsulated ceilings.

Transformer: device to change voltage.

Trim: various fittings for apertures.

Troffer: recessed fixture, usually fluorescent.

Tube: hollow cylinder with low-voltage lamp holders or fluorescent lamp.

UL: Underwriters Laboratories, a nonprofit organization that tests and approves fixtures that conform to national safety standards.

Wall Washer: fixture that redirects light at the wall.

Other Ready-Made, Not-So-Visible Fixtures

Several other ready-made, not-so-visible fixtures are available. The most spectacular are low-voltage strips and edge-lit fiber optics. The easiest to install are fluorescent brackets, coves, valances, cornices and canopies, or low-voltage cornices.

Ready-Made, Not-So-Visible Fixtures

- fluorescent skylights and troffers
- fluorescent integrated into upper cabinets
- low-voltage coves
- low-voltage strips

FLUORESCENT SKYLIGHTS AND TROFFERS

Large recessed fluorescent skylights, flat, sloped, or domed, create a window-like effect in kitchens and baths. They must be framed in during construction because of their size. They are unmatched in creating a light, airy space but cannot replace task lighting. They look best over tubs, whirlpools, kitchen islands, or other fittings.

In addition, fluorescent troffers are ready-made solutions for downlight. Their sizes are usually 2 feet by 4 feet, but can be 1 by 4, or 2 by 2, or 4 by 4. Their only drawback is that they impart a high-tech appearance. Some interior styles can tolerate the look. For styles that cannot, obscure the fixtures with decorative features: cloth baffles,

Large fluorescent fixture creates a skylight effect.

Siematic

paper umbrellas, banners, or other creative means.

FLUORESCENT INTEGRATED INTO UPPER CABINETS

Some cabinet manufacturers have recessed fluorescent fixtures into their upper cabinets. If the cabinets are suitable, use them. They solve the problem of hiding fixtures and do it energy efficiently with compact fluorescent.

LOW VOLTAGE

Low voltage for not-so-visible installation is available in different forms: tubes, tapes, or strips. The tubes, rigid or flexible, encase low-voltage lamps. Tubes can be easily glued or double-sticky taped to surfaces, either hidden or visible. They can illuminate from under ceramic tile overhangs in the bathroom. They can be tucked in handrails. Or they can be behind the overhang of stair treads, thereby lighting risers. Use them to illuminate a single step (an architectural "no-no" destined to trip everyone eventually). In addition, they can be under the platform of a raised hot tub or whirlpool, or under base cabinets in the toe space.

The tapes (sometimes called channels) have a row of low-voltage lamps in sockets. Tapes can be attached with double-sticky tape

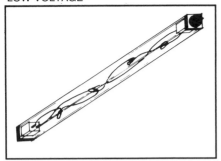

Tube.

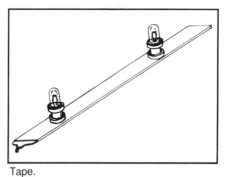

Tape.

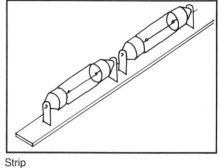

Strip

or screwed to the architecture or furnishings. They can give low-intensity cove lighting or can outline unusual architectural features. Also, they can illuminate bathroom shelves holding luxuriously colorful towels.

The strips are small right angles of aluminum that tuck behind small edges to hide the lamps. Some strips are self-sustaining with built-in transformers and switches on the fixture. They can be hard wired or plugged in. All are a boon to getting low-wattage light in small places.

Lamp sizes for tubes, tapes, and strips vary from ¼ to 10 watts. Some lamps are rated to last at 6,000 hours; some claimed at 100,000. Tape lamps are replaceable. Some tubes permit lamp replacements; many do not. Like all lamps, low-voltage eventually burns out. Consequently, replaceable tube lamps are best. Otherwise, the tube must be shipped back to the factory if under warranty, or replaced entirely. Unfortunately, most people wait until all the lamps are burned out before they seek replacements. But in the meantime, the intended visual effect has long gone. Not good!

Determine the spacing of the lamps. Typically, the spacing is 2, 3, 4, 6, or 12 inches. The closer together and the higher the wattage, the brighter the light is. If the space is bright, the low-voltage light must also be bright to be seen. However, the more lamps, the more heat is put out. In kitchens, unnecessary heat is not welcomed, particularly at countertops.

Low-voltage fixtures require a step-down transformer to reduce the line voltage (120) to low voltage (6, 12, or 24). Match the voltage to the lamp. Determine the transformer size by totalling the watts consumed by the lamps and adding an additional 20 percent. Choose a UL approved transformer. Install a fuse between the transformer and the low-voltage lamps. Dim only if absolutely necessary. Use a low-voltage dimmer. (See *Low Voltage* in Chapter 6.)

A recess of 1 inch is required to hide low-voltage tubes at stairs, countertops, and toe spaces. Low-voltage coves should not be more than 8 inches down from the ceiling and can be tucked into 45-degree angled molding. Toe spaces or risers should not be higher than 12 inches to be effectively lighted. Low-voltage strips can be installed in many places where no other fixture could be. The effect is exquisite, and the energy consumption is low.

In addition, ready-made cove moldings contain low-voltage fixtures. If mounted 8 inches or less from the ceiling, they can provide soft light.

Custom-Made, Not-So-Visible Fixtures

The second group of not-so-visible fixtures are custom made and built-in. They are composed of a light source and some method of holding the fixture up. The edge-lit fiber optics in glass blocks are installed by a mason. All the others are built by a carpenter. The carpenter-built fixtures are painted matte white inside to reflect as much light as possible. The exterior of the shielding can be finished to match the interior style. They require carpentry and sometimes plastering. The sources are usually linear and can be incandescent (hot and inefficient), fluorescent, or cold cathode (both cool, efficient, and in many colors), but could be a single source, MR, with prismatic material as the diffuser. The prismatic material can be either light weight, flexible film or medium weight and rigid. Either are delicate and the prism surface can be scratched. Both spread light evenly on the surface with assistance from a matte-white reflector around corners and a mirror at the end. Their ability to spread the light is outstanding. Both have excellent applications for kitchens and baths.

Between fluorescent and incandescent, fluorescent is best. The custom-made fixture can deliver light up, up and down, or down. Reflectors can further enhance delivery in a specific direction. The light distribution of custom-made fixtures is controlled by the design (shielding height, position of lamps, reflectors, etc.).

Custom-Made, Built-In, Not-So-Visible Fixtures

- arch reveals or recess lighting
- brackets
- canopies
- cornices
- coves
- dropped soffits
- edge-lit fiber optics
- luminous panels
- recessed perimeter coffers
- valances

Arch recess lighting.

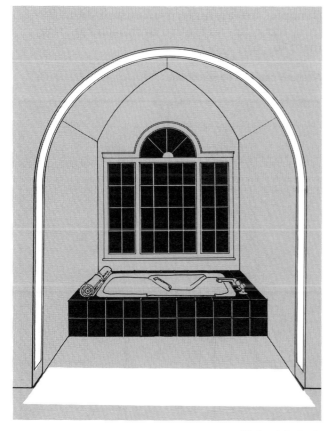

National Cathode

ARCH REVEALS OR RECESS LIGHTING

Often, divider walls in baths have no doors. The reveal (the sides of the opening) could have a light source behind a diffuser. The diffuser rises from the floor to the top of the doorway, and back down to the floor, carrying continuous light. It is as wide as the thickness of the wall. Choose to use an MR and prismatic material, or cold cathode and opal diffuser. Prismatic materials requires matte-white reflectors and mirrors to spread light evenly from the single source throughout the prismatic diffuser. Cold cathode illuminates softly; no other source can do it so well. Lamps last 20,000 hours, and the arch lighting gives a spectacular effect.

Likewise, recessed sidewalls in a vanity closet or vanity countertop can be side lighted with a diffuser from the countertop up across the ceiling and back down to the countertop. Use either cold cathode with an opal diffuser or a single MR lamp with prismatic material. Do not neglect this opportunity for lighting a recess or reveal.

BRACKETS

Brackets hang on the wall providing up- and/or downlight. They can illuminate architecturally from difficult places. A bracket can give both up- and downlight in a toilet recess or above a vanity mirror. It should be the same width as the recess or the mirror. Or it can give downlight only at an eating bar facing a wall. If the light source is not a single MR and prismatic material, the source should be linear and preferably fluorescent. Mount it on the wall. The faceboard needs to obscure the view of the light source from the typical positions in the space—seated or standing. Brackets are designed to look correct with the architecture and work with the modules of linear lighting. Fluorescent sources can be used. Use the 1- or 1½-inch (T8 or T12) fluorescent lamp in 3- or 4-foot sizes. Use the rapid-start type and avoid the flick, flick, flick when turned on. If brackets do not go from wall to wall, box in the ends with a return (like a drapery return). The return holds the light in. Normally, brackets are open at the top and bottom. But in some positions, a lens or louver is necessary to block the view of the lamp. Lenses or louvers are particularly useful in kitchen banquettes and other close-to-the-wall seating areas.

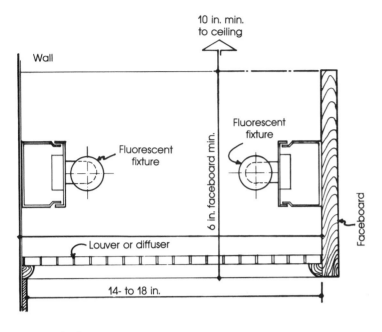

10 in. min. to ceiling

Wall

Fluorescent fixture

6 in. faceboard min.

Fluorescent fixture

Faceboard

Louver or diffuser

14- to 18 in.

Bracket details.

Bracket Installation

1. Install the bracket at least 10 inches down from the ceiling to allow adequate reflection.
2. Make the bracket 14 to 18 inches deep.
3. Place the faceboard at least 6 inches high and covered with any material that enhances the interior decor—wood, tiles, wallpaper, fabric, or paint.
4. Use two single fluorescent lamps—one on the inside of the faceboard and one on the wall.
5. Fit the fixture between the ends of the bracket in order to have a smooth wash of light.
6. Paint the inside of the faceboard matte white.
7. Use a lens or louver at the bottom, if necessary.
8. Use white perforated metal on the top, covering just the fluorescent lamp at the wall or covering both lamps for less light on the ceiling, if desirable.

CANOPIES

Canopy fixtures are suspended from the ceiling and provide up- and/or downlight. If they are to provide uplight, they must be at least 10 inches down from the ceiling. They are particularly good over kitchen islands and other base cabinets or, if cleverly designed, over pedestal lavatories in the bathroom. Over kitchen islands, the louvers can be slats of wood from which pots and pans can be hung. The fluorescent fixtures are mounted on the inside of the faceboard around the perimeter

of the canopy. A lens blocks the view of the lamps. A louver obscures the view from a 45° angle, the standard viewing angle in a space. Obviously, other viewing angles occur regularly, but louvers allow direct light down to the work surface. Take your choice.

A canopy is a wooden frame, open above and covered with a lens or louver below. The light from the fluorescent lamps bounces off the ceiling and down through the lens or louver. Make the canopy proportional to the cabinets below and within the sizes of fluorescent fixtures (multiples of 3 or 4 feet). Suspend it 10 inches from the ceiling in an average-height room, lower in a higher ceiling. Make the depth of the canopy at least 6 inches. Fluorescent fixtures can be mounted at the sides of the canopy or if a lens is used, in a row from side to side. If side by side, the distance between the fixtures should be one-and-a-half times the depth of the frame. The distance from a fixture to the side of the frame should be half the distance between the fixtures. Therefore, if the frame is 6 inches deep, the fixtures should be 9 inches apart.

Linear incandescent sources can also be used, but produce possibly unwelcome heat. Canopies are an underused custom-built fixture and offer a creative architectural statement for any space.

A canopy puts light up and down.

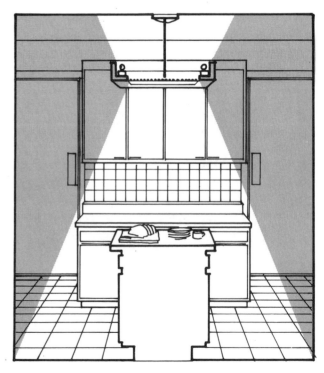

Canopy Installation over a Kitchen Island

1. Build a wooden frame canopy to complement the size of the kitchen island.
2. Suspend it at least 10 inches down from the ceiling. Use hollow tubing for the wires or recess the wiring in wooden suspension boards. Lower is more visually effective.
3. Make the side at least 4½ inches deep to hide the fluorescent fixtures and a 3½-inch return at the bottom to hold the fixtures along two sides.
4. Install asymmetric reflectors behind the fluorescent lamps for the maximum amount of light on ceiling.
5. Use a prismatic or opal lens on the bottom and keep the top open.

CORNICES

Cornices are mounted at the top of the wall. They are usually wall to wall but can also connect upper cabinets. Like other built-in fixtures (unless single-source MR and prismatic material are used) linear lamps fit the best. Use 1- or 1½-inch (T8 or T12) fluorescent lamps. Fixtures are mounted on the ceiling and the opening is covered with a lens or louver. Lenses appear bright; louvers can appear dark, if parabolic. Egg-crate louvers (less expensive than parabolic) are somewhat bright. Lenses obscure the view of the lamp from all angles. Louvers, since they have openings, cannot block completely. Take your choice. Cornice boards can be finished with special wall coverings in kitchens and baths.

Fluorescent cornices are excellent for all styles of interiors, but particularly for period-style interiors and traditional furnishings, which are normally difficult to combine with fluorescent lighting. They are also sleek and tasteful in contemporary interiors.

A cornice, if properly installed, obscures the light sources and does not attract attention to itself. It focuses on the wall. This system can accommodate ceilings that slope away from a wall, provided the wall height is even. The fluorescent light goes about halfway down the wall, trailing off in brightness.

If other light sources in the room are incandescent, choose the kind of fluorescent lamp that puts out a compatible color of light (around 30°K). Otherwise, the colors will fight. Also, the color must flatter the occupants. Cool white, commonly used in offices, will not be flattering. Warm-white, warm-white deluxe, or prime-color fluorescent will. In addition, use all the same type color lamps in the cornice to provide a uniform color on the wall. If one lamp color is changed, change them all.

Since the 3- and 4-foot fluorescent fixtures are the most common, use them. They are easy to obtain but not every wall is divisible by either 3 or 4. Two sizes might be needed. For example, a 15-foot wall could not accommodate only 4-foot fixtures. Use three 4-foot fixtures and one 3-foot fixture.

Be aware that only the 3- and 4-foot rapid-start fixtures can be dimmed. The instant or preheated fixtures cannot. However, dimming is usually not necessary because fluorescent light is already low in wattage. Likewise, fluorescent fixtures do not usually create unpleasant brightness if the installation is designed well.

Place the fixtures end to end, within the limits of the fixture sizes. Normally, some empty space is left over, but keep it to a minimum and equalize it at each end. Or if more than a minimum space is left, equalize it by separating each fixture by an inch or so, using up the extra inches. However, be aware that empty spaces between fixtures create shadows that destroy the smooth-wash effect.

Cornice Installation for a Wall

1. Make a faceboard of hardboard or plywood no less than 6 inches deep and as long as the wall being lighted.
2. Prevent the lamps from being seen from a usual position in the room—seated or standing—by using a narrow return added to the bottom of the board. The return could hold a lens or louver to further hide the lamp.
3. Paint the inside of the board matte, not glossy, white.
4. Attach the board to the ceiling at least 6 inches out from the wall.
5. Mount the fixtures on the ceiling next to the board either on 1-by-3-inch wooden blocks or directly behind the board if decorative molding is to be attached on the outside at the top. Either way, the light cannot leak out at the top of the faceboard.
6. Paint, stain, cover, or plaster the outside of the cornice board. Use whatever enhances the style of the room and blends with the wall covering.
7. Modify the measurements of the depth of the cornice board by the proportions of the board to the space, the view under the board, and other architectural considerations. Also, modify the measurements of distance from the wall by considering how far you want the light to be thrown down on the wall.

The farther the fixtures are installed from the wall, the farther down the wall the light will be thrown. In fact, for each 1 foot out from the wall, the light will go down 4 feet. If you want light on the visible wall above cabinets or furniture, install the fixtures only 1 foot out.

When building, a cornice system can be preplanned and the wiring provided. The cornice board can be made to match the other woodwork, especially if it is distinctive.

When relighting, a cornice system can be installed if wires are available either from access through the attic, a hot switch, or a baseboard receptacle. Skilled electricians often can reach wires in wooden frame construction but not so often in other types.

The light will spread as far as the fixtures are spread—ideally from end to end. More light will be at the top of the wall than at the bottom, but it will be bright and pleasing. The amount reflected into the room will be rich and glowing, sufficient to read the weather forecast but not enough to read the whole newspaper.

A cornice board between upper cabinets can hide a fixture.

St. Charles

A cornice can also be a cornice board connecting upper cabinets and hiding a light fixture. This choice is excellent for over kitchen sinks. The board can conceal a surface-mounted or recessed incandescent fixture, low-voltage preferably, to create strong and direct downlight for kitchen tasks. Use a 50-watt MR16 narrow flood or a 36-watt PAR wide flood. For an inexpensive installation, use a porcelain socket and a 75-watt elliptical reflector, which gives as much light as a 150-watt line-voltage incandescent.

On the other hand, a leaded-glass panel can be the cornice (or face) board and create a luminous panel between the upper cabinets while putting light down on the kitchen sink. (See *Luminous Panels* in this chapter.)

Sample Electric Cost

A fluorescent system for a 16-foot wall using four 4-foot lamps of 40 watts each requires 160 watts for the lamps and 24 watts for the ballast. Used for 4 hours per night at 10¢ per kilowatt-hour, it costs $2.21 for a month. Fluorescent lamps last up to 20 times as long as incandescent, and they spread light farther. In addition, they create a lot less heat. The overall savings—fewer watts for lighting and less cooling by fan or air conditioner in hot weather—would offset the slightly higher installation cost of the fluorescent system.

COVES

A cove uplights for general room illumination in a bathroom or kitchen. Cove light can come from a plaster recess in the center of the ceiling, from a carpenter-built, wooden device mounted on one or more walls, or from fixtures on top of upper cabinets. Either way, the ceiling is bright and reflects light into the whole room. A center-ceiling cove can be straight sided, partially curved, or dome shaped. A cove along the walls or above cabinets is usually rectilinear. Light sources are tucked behind the faceboard. Many sources are available. Choice of light source depends upon the geometry of the cove. Curved coves require continuous curved coverage. A single MR source and prismatic material meet this criterion. Likewise, so does neon, cold cathode, and low-voltage strips. When the cove is straight sided, 1-inch fluorescent fixtures in modules of 3- or 4-foot lengths, if modules fit without gaps, can be used. Be aware that gaps between fixtures create shadows that destroy the smooth-wash effect of the light on the

Coves give general illumination.

St. Charles

ceiling. Coves are energy-efficient, general illumination in kitchens and baths. In a center-ceiling cove, their appearance can be punctuated by a hanging decorative fixture, adding additional uplight, if desired.

In kitchens, typically cove installations are on the top of upper cabinets that do not go all the way to the ceiling. Whether ready-made or custom-made cabinets, a faceboard to shield the lighting is easy to add.

Cove Installation on Upper Cabinets

1. Position upper cabinets at least 10 inches down from the ceiling. The further down, the greater the throw of light.
2. Install the fluorescent fixture on blocking with the center of the lamp about 5 inches from the wall and at least 2 inches back from the faceboard. The blocking can be angled 20 degrees, or an asymmetric reflector can throw the light.
3. Make the faceboard high enough to obscure the view of the lamps, usually 4 inches.
4. Paint the inside of the board matte white.
5. Use metal brackets, if cold cathode, neon, or low-voltage strips are used; do not install on blocking. Likewise, install the transformer in an accessible, but remote location to reduce any transformer noise.

Make sure the faceboard is just high enough to obscure seeing the light sources. Higher reduces the light available to reflect off the ceiling. Faceboards can match the other woodwork in the space, especially if distinctive. When remodeling, a cove can be installed if wires are available in the ceiling or from adjacent spaces, including closets.

In both kitchens and baths, coves can be along one or more walls of the room. For general distribution, use coves on two or more walls. Coves can throw light to sloping or flat ceilings. Do not install a cove closer than 10 inches from the ceiling surface. Otherwise, a hot line of light will be reflected with little light spread. To thrust the light towards the center of the ceiling, either angle the faceboard, angle the fixtures, or install an asymmetric reflector behind the fluorescent lamp.

Rule of Thumb for Light Spread by Coves

Cove on one side of the space
SPREAD OF LIGHT = DD ÷ .25

Cove on opposite sides of the space
SPREAD OF LIGHT = DD ÷ .15

Cove section.

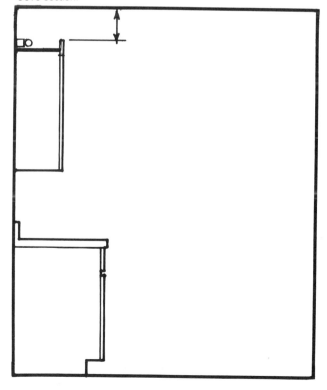

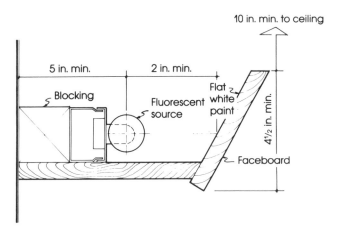

Cove details.

Dropped soffit.

Be sure to have coves dusted when the room is dusted. Light is diminished by dust and the cove surfaces are just as dust prone as any surface. Never light a windowless space with only a cove. The visual impression is like a dreary overcast day. Complement cove light with the brilliance of downlight and/or daylight.

DROPPED SOFFITS

A portion of the ceiling dropped down is called a dropped soffit. Similar to a cornice, a soffit gives downlight only. In kitchens, soffits are used above and in front of upper cabinets that do not go to the ceiling. In baths, soffits are also used above a vanity countertop, preferably between two side walls. Any type of soffit is highly successful.

With textured upper cabinets in a kitchen, use recessed, incandescent, open downlights in the soffit. Open downlights over the upper cabinets can provide grazing light to enhance the texture in upper cabinet doors. The soffit can be carried over the sink between upper cabinets and provide downlight for the brightest illumination. Soffits are dropped the distance available above the upper cabinets, usually 7 or more inches deep. A soffit is the most successful way of lighting inside the upper cabinets but it does not replace countertop lighting. Soffit light cannot get to the back of the counter. Use incandescent fixtures only when needing to enhance texture or getting good light at the sink. Otherwise, use fluorescent.

Without upper cabinets in either a bath or kitchen, a soffit should be the same length (left to right) as the vanity or countertop, but not the same depth (front to back). Soffits are usually dropped 12 or more inches and are 18 inches deep. Linear fluorescent fixtures are the best. The fixtures are mounted on the ceiling inside the soffit, and a lens or louver obscures the view. Lenses are bright visual elements. Louvers are not. Do not use a parabolic louver over kitchen cabinets. It sends the light down and would not light the inside of the upper kitchen cabinets. The faceboard is usually plastered and finished like the adjacent walls.

Dropped Soffit Installation Over Vanity Tops

1. Box in an area of a ceiling, dropping it 8 to 12 inches down.
2. Make it 12 to 18 inches deep, sufficient to hold a lens or louver to scatter the light.
3. Make it as wide as the cabinets below.
4. Use two single or a double fluorescent fixture mounted on the ceiling, unless the room has medium- to dark-colored walls or unless your client's eyes require more light. If so, use three or four fluorescent lamps or install a reflector behind each lamp.
5. Paint the inside of the soffit matte white to reflect as much light as possible.
6. Build a small return at the opening of the soffit to hold a lens or louver that can be tilted for removal. In small bathrooms, louvers are best, because they do not pop up and down with the door opening and closing.

7. The exterior surface of the soffit should be finished to blend with the walls, and the lens or louver color should blend with the ceiling. For example, a dropped soffit could be built of sheetrock, plastered, painted off-white on the bottom to match the ceiling, and wallpapered on the outside to match the walls.

Dropped soffits are the excellent fixtures for lighting inside kitchen upper cabinets. An ample amount of light can be provided and the distribution is broad enough to reach into upper cabinets. Likewise, dropped soffits are the excellent fixtures for lighting faces at bathroom mirrors. With fluorescent sources, they avoid facial shadows that make grooming difficult. In kitchens or baths, they can provide ample light with little glare. Their installation expense is repaid by the slick architectural look and the good light distribution. (They look best when constructed wall to wall, rather then a small section of the ceiling dropped.) They impart no particular style statement, since they are built in. Hence they can be combined with any interior decor.

EDGE-LIT FIBER OPTICS

Edge-lit fiber optics can light glass or plastic blocks in kitchens and baths. The fibers are made of a material that carry the light from

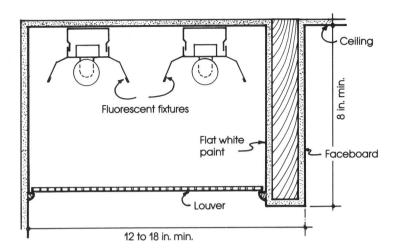

Soffit details.

the MR (or metal-halide) lamp to the blocks. For glass blocks, square fibers can be mortared on the surface between the edges of the blocks. Oval fibers can be embedded in clear mortar between the glass blocks. Plastic blocks are not mortared, but are interlocked leaving a hollow opening. Oval or square fibers can be threaded into the opening. Surface fibers are brighter, but they are geometric—linear and/or vertical. Internal fibers bounce light off facets or uneven planes of the blocks.

Fiber optics between blocks.

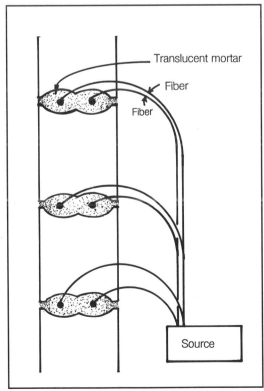

Fiber Lite

Fiber optics at edges.

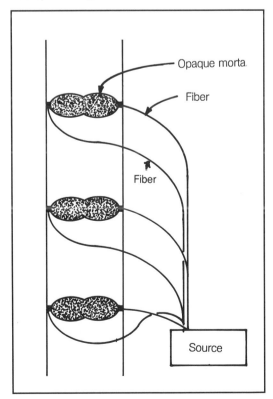

Blocks can be facetted with ribbing, cut-glass patterns, or wavy distortions. Choose blocks that have many facets to catch light. The more facets, the more places for the light to reflect. For color, choose colored blocks or have fiber optics deliver color with a filter or color wheel at the light box between the lamp and the fiber optics.

See for Yourself #6: How Light Behaves with Glass

1. Find a smooth glass tumbler.
2. Shine a flashlight through it.
3. Observe the glass and see where the glass catches the light.
4. Find a cut-glass object and shine a light through it.
5. Observe the glass and see where the glass catches the light.

When light passes through glass or plastic, it passes straight through unless there is a facet to catch and reflect it. Blocks have different surface textures to catch light. Some are geometric; others are wavy. If using clear blocks, construct the lighting like a luminous panel. Clear blocks need a panel to scatter the light from hidden sources.

LUMINOUS PANELS

Luminous panels between the countertop and the upper cabinet can be a backsplash, or between two upper cabinets can be a cornice. Both provide not only light but also a decorative ambience. The panels can be glass or plastic. The idea is to create lighted surfaces behind the glass that scatter and reflect the light. If the panel is transparent, do not have light sources directly behind it; the source can be seen. If sources cannot be hidden, use prismatic film. If the panel is translucent, light sources can be directly behind; the source cannot be seen.

As the backsplash, choose panel colors that do not impart a distinct hue to the light. Red, green, or blue, for example, would make food look odd. For the cornice position, choose any hue. The light below will still be white, and the light transmitted through the panel will be colorful without causing interference. Light sources can be fluorescent or, if a continuous source is needed, cold cathode. As the backsplash, a panel should be illuminated by fluorescent fixtures or a single MR source and prismatic material.

Fiber-optics lighting glass blocks.

Cornice luminous panel.

Luminous Panel Installation

1. Build a box for the fluorescent channels. Place them at the top and bottom, or at the left and right sides, 4 inches back from the edges so that they will not show.
2. Make the box one-sixth as deep as the distance between the channels, to obtain even light. For example, if the channels are 21 inches apart, the box depth could be 3½ inches.
3. Paint the inside of the box matte white.
4. Hinge the panel so that the lamps can be replaced when they burn out, usually not sooner than three years.
5. Plan how to control the luminous panel; a wall switch is the most convenient to use.

If the cornice board above the kitchen sink is a leaded-glass luminous panel, use surface-mounted fluorescent fixtures well back from the sides of the panel. The 18-inch linear or 27-watt compact fluorescent are good choices. The light needs to be well scattered to effectively light the leaded glass and put light directly below. Paint the surfaces behind the cornice matte white. Design the leaded-glass panel when the cornice is designed to accommodate the fixtures.

RECESSED PERIMETER COFFER

A recessed perimeter coffer is framed and recessed when the walls are built. It is at the ceiling/wall edge and accepts manufactured fixtures. It is plastered or finished like the rest of the walls. The interior is painted matte white and there is no faceboard, since it is recessed into the ceiling. Perimeter coffers can hold a track-lighting system for strong incandescent light. This choice is especially good for highly textured masonry walls. Or they can hold fluorescent, cold cathode, or prismatic material and a single MR source. This choice is suitable for nontextured walls. Both incandescent and fluorescent systems are available. Incandescent can be track lights or a single MR source. Track lights would give shadows for textured walls. With nontextured walls, use energy-efficient fluorescent with open, prismatic lens, baffle, or louvers, or an MR with prismatic material. Install along one or more walls in a continuous run. Typically, the fluorescent units are the standard 2-, 3-, and 4-foot lengths. The prismatic material may be as long as needed and be uninterrupted.

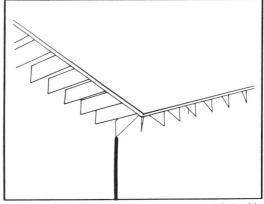

Recessed perimeter coffer.

Columbia

VALANCES

Valances are put at the top of windows. They can give up- and downlight over draperies or other window treatment. Often, large windows take up a large part of a wall. Sometimes these windows are covered with draperies and closed at night. The draperies become a major element in the space, contributing color and texture. Valance lighting not only reflects from the draperies, but also from the ceiling, giving the space greater illumination. Light drapes with a valance. If used over draperies, put the fixtures on blocking to bring the lamp in front of the draperies. Always keep the lamp 2 inches from any wood or cloth sur-

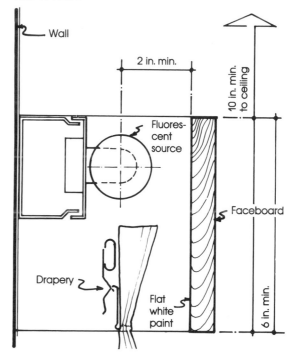

Valance details.

Wall

2 in. min.

Fluorescent source

10 in. min. to ceiling

Faceboard

Drapery

Flat white paint

6 in. min.

face, including the faceboard of the valance itself. They are effective in kitchen eating alcoves. Or valances can give uplight only above sliding glass doors in the bathroom. Valances can be used easily with sloped ceilings because they are installed well below the ceiling line.

If they are to provide uplight, they must be at least 10 inches down from the ceiling. Use 1- or 1½-inch (T8 or T12) fluorescent lamps. Unless the faceboard is wall to wall, build returns at the ends. Like brackets, valances normally do not have a lens or louver at the bottom opening, but they might be necessary above sliding glass doors. If one portion of the valance needs a lens, all portions must have a lens.

A valance is basically like a cornice but is installed on the wall.

Valance Installation over Draperies

1. Install faceboard a minimum of 10 inches from the ceiling to let enough light out.
2. Position the lamp at least 2 inches away from the faceboard and the draperies to dissipate the heat.
3. Make the faceboard at least 6 inches deep, or deeper as required to conceal the lamps from people seated.
4. Paint the board matte white inside to reflect as much light as possible.
5. Position the board at least 4½ inches out from the wall for clearance.
6. Position the lamp at least 2 inches up from the bottom of the faceboard to conceal it.
7. Install the fluorescent fixture on 2-by-3-inch wood blocking.
8. Smoothly spread the light for the whole length of the drapes.
9. Choose fluorescent (preferably) or linear incandescent.
10. Build returns to obscure the light fixtures and complete the valance, if the draperies do not cover the whole wall end to end.
11. Hold the faceboard to the wall with ½-inch metal or wooden angle brackets.
12. Finish the board to harmonize or contrast with the interior design of the space.

Lamps for valances can be either fluorescent or incandescent. For those who do not like fluorescent, linear incandescent is available (with its disadvantages). Linear incandescent has been popular in Europe. Linear length and wattage are interrelated. The three sizes are: 12 inches at 35 watts, 20 inches at 60 watts, and 40 inches at 120 watts. They can be mounted end to end behind faceboards. (They can also be mounted visibly without faceboards for other lighting uses.) Further, they can easily be dimmed. But they are not energy efficient. Use only when fluorescent will not do.

Valance light will be soft and appealing. The amount of illumination depends upon the color of the surfaces it lights, the wattage of the lamps, and the light in the rest of the space. It will permit easy-to-see activities, such as setting a table, eating an informal meal, or exercising. It will spread as wide as the fixtures are spread.

Light Distribution of Custom-Made Fixtures

UPLIGHT

cove	valance	canopy
bracket		

UP- AND DOWNLIGHT

bracket	valance	canopy
luminous panel		

DOWNLIGHT

bracket	valance	canopy
dropped soffit	cornice	recessed
		perimeter coffer

SIDELIGHT

arch reveal
recess

Custom-made lighting is clearly an excellent choice. It fits the module of the architecture and/or the cabinets. It blends in and delivers light unnoticeably. Preplanning is necessary in the early stages of the structure's design. It is worth the trouble.

Custom-Made, Not-So-Visible Fixture Vocabulary

Arch Lighting: lighting installed behind a diffuser in the reveal of a doorway.

Bracket Lighting: a lighted wall-hung unit.

Canopy Lighting: a fixture suspended from the ceiling over a countertop or other counter-height unit.

Coffer: a recessed panel in the ceiling.

Cornice Lighting: molding or other woodwork on the wall at the ceiling hiding downlights.

Cove Lighting: 1. a lighted recess in the ceiling, which can be straight sided, partially curved, or dome shaped. 2. a lighted, custom-made board mounted near the top of the wall. 3. fixtures providing light from the top of tall furniture or upper cabinets.

Dropped-Soffit Lighting: a lighted portion of the ceiling dropped down in front of upper cabinets.

Edge-Lit Fiber Optics: fibers that transmit the light from the sides of the fibers.

Luminous Panel: Lighted transluscent or clear panels on the ceiling, as a cornice or a backsplash.

Recess Lighting: lighting installed behind a diffuser in a countertop or closet vanity alcove.

Recessed Perimeter Coffer: a recess holding fixtures at the ceiling along one or more walls.

Reveal: the thickness of the wall in the sides of an opening.

Valance Lighting: a lighted decorative header over windows, particularly with draperies.

visible

Fixtures that are visible are either functional or decorative. On the one hand, functional fixtures are surface-mounted versions of recessed fixtures or are manufactured versions of custom-made fixtures. On the other hand, decorative fixtures are lighting jewelry and chosen because of style. They can be custom designed, but should be UL (Underwriters Laboratories) approved. Otherwise, if something goes wrong, a fire or an electric shock is possible.

Functional Fixtures

Functional fixtures are surface mounted on or suspended from the ceiling, on the wall, or under upper cabinets.

Functional Fixtures

- accent
- brackets
- canopies
- ceiling mounted or ceiling suspended
- cornices
- coves
- downlights
- linear incandescent
- porcelain socket
- perimeter fluorescent
- track
- upper-cabinet mount
- valances
- wall washers

Surface mounted.

ACCENT, DOWNLIGHT, AND WALL-WASHER FIXTURES

Downlights, wall-washers, and accent fixtures can be semirecessed, surface mounted, or suspended from the ceiling. Like decorative pendants, they are particularly good in high ceilings. Also, they are excellent alternatives when recessing is not possible. But, like any visible fixture, they are always in view. In 8-foot ceilings, they can clutter, detracting from the design intent. Design carefully. (Consult descriptions of the various fixtures in the *Recessed Fixture Vocabulary* in this chapter.)

FLUORESCENT FIXTURES

Many ready-made fluorescent fixtures are available and can be used in numerous places in kitchens and baths. In kitchens, a ceiling-mounted fluorescent fixture over an island or a peninsula is often a good choice for general lighting. They can match most any decor. In baths with exercise spaces and mirrored walls, fluorescent surface mounted around the perimeter provides glare-free light. In both kitchens or baths, suspended fluorescent in a continuous run over base cabinets can distribute task light either directly down or up and reflecting down.

Further, ready-made bracket, canopy, cornice, cove, and valance fixtures are also fluorescent. The ones that use the 1-inch, T8 lamp have a small 3-inch profile. Various lenses, louvers, or diffusers are available to distribute the light as intended. Fixtures are available in luscious colors and special colors can be ordered. Typical lengths are 2, 3, 4, 6, and 8 feet. They are good alternatives when custom-made, not-so-visible lighting is impossible.

A canopy can be made by ceiling-suspended fluorescent uplights tandem mounted.

LiteControl

Alkco

They look appropriate in a square or rectangular shape above a base cabinet or island. If the ceiling is 8 feet, make sure that the fixture is engineered to spread the light and not create hot spots. (Most fluorescent uplights cannot spread light well in 8-foot ceilings.) Well-engineered uplights create excellent general illumination and the fixtures are available in many colors.

Ready-made fixtures are available that resemble trims—half-round or crown molding. The half-round is about 4 inches high and protrudes 2½ inches. The crown is about 5½ inches high and protrudes 5 inches. Two fluorescent lamps are in the fixtures. They can be used in bracket or cove positions. Fixtures can be continuous and are made in seventy colors.

Many upper-cabinet fixtures designed for countertop lighting are well engineered. Some are not. One well-engineered fixture gives an option for left- or right-hand lamp positions for glare-free countertop or kitchen desk lighting. Another has two levels of light, useful for difficult visual tasks or for older eyes. Some have solid fronts to create a built-in shield.

These fixtures are valuable for ready-made cabinets that have no place to hide the fixture.

Perimeter fluorescent light is obtainable by surface, tandem-mounted fluorescent fixtures along one or more walls. They fit well architecturally if the module, usually the 3- or 4-foot, works with the length of the walls. They should go wall to wall.

LINEAR INCANDESCENT FIXTURES

Yes, incandescent lamps can be linear and can be mounted on the surface. They create a warm line of light. They can be inexpensively dimmed. The lamp is mounted on a small base that is architectural. Like linear fluorescent lamps, their wattages are linked to their length. The three sizes are: 12 inches at 35 watts, 20 inches at 60 watts, and 40 inches at 150 watts. They can be mounted end to end, if desirable. The lamps, however, are in full view when lighted. In spaces with little additional light, they can be glaring. Plan their use wisely.

PORCELAIN SOCKET

The least expensive fixture is a porcelain or keyless socket. It holds any screw-base, line-voltage lamp, but it should be installed well out of sight or above eye level. Use them for inexpensive installations behind a cornice board over a sink or in a high-ceiling skylight in the bath with G lamps.

TRACK FIXTURES

The most popular surface-mounted fixtures are track. They are especially good for specifiers who cannot accurately determine recessed fixture placement or want aiming flexibility. Tracks adapt to interior changes, whereas recessed fixtures usually cannot. However, track fixtures are always in view. In small kitchens, line-voltage track heads clutter the space. Choose low-voltage heads for less clutter. Several manufacturers also make low-voltage chandeliers and pendants that hook up to their low-voltage track.

Low-voltage track fixtures hold MR16, T4, MR11, and PAR lamps in wattages from 20 to 75 and beam spreads from very narrow spot to very wide flood. The opportunities for superb lighting effects are limitless.

Decorative Fixtures

Decorative fixtures in kitchens and baths can be on the ceiling, on the wall, suspended from the ceiling, on tabletops, or on the floor. Typically in most residential spaces, the most numerous decorative fixtures are portable fixtures (table or floor lamps). Not so in kitchens and baths. (However, I have seen an interior designer's kitchen in South Florida that was lighted by only portable fixtures. It was pretty dark for tasks by most standards.)

Decorative Fixtures for Style

- chandeliers
- pendants
- portable fixtures
- wall or ceiling-surface fixtures
- bare-wire low-voltage fixtures

These decorative fixtures are jewelry. Their style, form, and physical presence cannot be ignored. Use them like you would use any jewelry—to enrich. Jewelry enriches clothing. Similarly, a decorative fixture enriches a room. Decorative fixtures can enrich by matching the room's style, by being different, or by creating the decorative statement.

Matching styles is safe.

Mixing styles takes skill.

Capri and Robert Long

Decorative fixtures can be the same style as the architecture and interiors. Thus, they carry out the decorative theme. Choosing the same style is safe: a period-style fixture with period-style furniture, a newly designed fixture with contemporary furniture, or a rustic fixture with Southwestern furniture.

Style types have many origins. Some are historic and named after a monarch (Queen Anne). Others are named after a furniture designer (Chippendale), have a religious foundation (Shaker), were a popular design movement (Art Nouveau), or are geographically based (Italian or Oriental). Finally, some reflect a theme or mood (nautical or rustic).

Without a doubt, when restoring architecture to its previous condition, decorative fixtures need to match the architectural style. Historic preservation is a worthwhile but time-consuming project. Happily, more lighting fixture manufacturers specialize in historic lighting fixtures. Often manufacturers make the fixtures as they would have long ago. Be sure that a testing laboratory has approved the fixture, then your fixture is up to current safety standards. Some state governments have specialists available to assist with selections that are consistent with the historic style.

Preserving Historic Architecture

Contacts for historic preservation specialists to find sources for matching lighting fixtures to architecture:

- your local Historic Society
- your state Historical Preservation Office

Decorative fixtures can be a different style than the architecture and interiors. This choice takes courage and requires a good eye for design. Sometimes, a traditional chandelier can successfully enrich a contemporary setting. However, vice versa is hard. Most contemporary chandeliers do not enrich a well-executed traditional setting: Queen Anne, Early American, Victorian, and other distinctive, easily recognized furniture styles. Somehow they clash. One exception is contemporary fixtures with Neoclassic furniture of smooth lines and geometric, rather than floral ornamentation. When deciding whether to choose a different style of decorative fixture, pretest your options. Pretest by drawing the fixture in a two-point perspective of the room, by scanning it into a CAD system, or by paste up on a photograph.

See for Yourself #7: How Will the Decorative Fixture Look?

Pretest how the decorative fixture will look by:
1. Taking a Polaroid snapshot of the room. Cutting out a picture or photocopy of the fixture from the catalog.
2. Reducing it on a copy machine until it is the right scale for the snapshot. (Use the wall height as your measuring line. For example, if the fixture is 2 feet wide, it should be one fourth as high as the 8-foot wall.)
3. Copying it on clear sticky-back paper, obtainable from architectural drafting-supply stores.
4. Cutting out the fixture in a square or circle. Peel off the backing and put on the snapshot. (The paper is clear and will not cover up the photograph.)
5. Judging whether you like it. You'll know.

Ready-made fixtures tandem mounted.

Raak

Decorative fixtures can create the decorative statement for a space. This choice is particularly useful when the interior decor is not strictly one style or another. For example, a chandelier with wrought-iron scroll branches and bobèches with pressed-glass drops in a guest bathroom sets the style for the space from beginning to end. Or a large, fragile Japanese paper lantern in an elegant, almost-Polynesian kitchen/greatroom sets the tone for subtle brocades and fine-grained furniture with elongated brass hardware. (I was going to use a paper lantern in such a room until I discovered that the client had a pet hawk that occasionally was allowed to fly around the house. Paper lanterns and sharp talons do not mix. A glass globe was substituted.)

Low voltage with exposed wires.

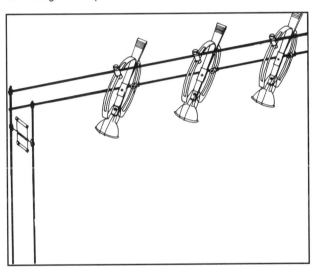

Translite

Decorative, ready-made wall fixtures can be tandem mounted to create a stylized line of light unequalled for impact. Although most of us have not done so, experiment with them. Many styles of wall fixtures are available to create artful combinations. Such efforts are warranted, particularly for the client who desires to be unique. (Most clients do.)

Low voltage is a safe voltage and fixtures can be strung on low-voltage wires without danger of shock. Usually, they are strung wall to wall, positioned close to the ceiling and/or dropping into the space at right angles or curves, making a look-at-me statement. The bare wires appear to be dangerous, but they are not. Use only UL listed transformers, wires, and fixtures. The low-voltage system

glitters and rightfully appears high tech. These systems are hard to design and should be cleverly installed to appear to come from nowhere. They are the most challenging lighting, and well worth the end product—a striking visual effect.

Sometimes, decorative fixtures are chosen to make a decorative statement reflecting an activity. For example, a leaded-glass pendant with ace of spades and jack of diamonds can be over a game table in a large kitchen/ family room for a card-playing client. (You can even have one custom made with your client's name.)

Leaded-glass pendant.

Match the mood of the space with the mood set by a decorative fixture. For example, use an outdoor lantern as an indoor wall fixture in a bathroom with lots of plants or where the decor is garden-like. Use a delicate, ornate chandelier hung centered on a gracious arched window at a kitchen eating area, enhancing the period-style or delicately scaled furniture.

Use a wooden chandelier over a wooden kitchen peninsula or island. Use a library pendant (a double fixture) over rectangular, counter-height base cabinets with no upper cabinets. Use an etched-glass, Art Nouveau fixture over a divider between an Art Nouveau living room and kitchen. Such placement enhances not only aesthetically, but also visually with more light for the task. Two benefits come from one fixture.

Use a polished-chrome, surgeon's pendant in a cool minimalist bathroom that could show off such a massive spotlight fixture. Use a rusted iron and glass-globe chandelier with a downlight over a kitchen eating table in a monochromatic, beams-and-brick kitchen.

A contemporary ceiling fixture gives a chandelier-like effect.

Spacious kitchens or baths look good with a hanging decorative fixture and a matching wall-mounted fixture. Use a contemporary uplight pendant with matching wall-mounted fixture. Use a contemporary uplight pendant with matching wall fixture in a contemporary kitchen seating area for soft light. Use chandeliers with candelabra wall sconces or glass-rod pendants with glass-rod wall fixtures. The repeated style ties the decorative scheme together reinforcing the effect.

A contemporary ceiling fixture becomes a chandelier when centered over an eating table or peninsula. Do not neglect these fixtures as a possibility for effective lighting jewelry.

PLACES FOR DECORATIVE FIXTURES

A hanging decorative fixture can emphasize the eating area in a kitchen/family room with a distinctive vertical accent. Similarly, furniture (tables, desks, sideboards, or chest of drawers) or cabinetwork (islands, peninsula, or other table-height base cabinets) can be emphasized. Further, kitchen or bath fireplaces are enhanced by a pendant or chandelier hung asymmetrically. The massiveness and verticalness are intensified. From both inside and out, a vertical window can frame a hanging fixture, creating an architectural surprise from the outside. Cove recesses, straight sided, partially curved, or domed, are brought into focus with a chandelier or uplight pendant hung in the center. The cove or dome can be glossy in finish if the lighting sources will not reflect in the finish. Uplight pendants can increase the amount of ceiling-reflected illumination, while making a decorative statement.

Be careful of high ceilings in small kitchens and bathrooms. If a hanging fixture is desirable, consider positioning it off center rather than dead center on the ceiling. Dead center tends to make the room appear smaller. Instead, hang it off center to counter-height cabinets or furniture.

A chandelier seen through a window ...

...creates a pleasing architectural surprise.

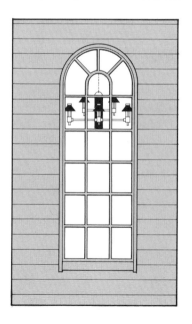

Uplight can create a harsh line.

Several pendants creates a rhythm.

Wall-mounted uplights can focus on arched or high sloped ceilings. However, never use only wall-mounted uplights with opaque shades. They can create a harsh line around the walls of the room with brightness above and dimness below. Not good! Alter the distribution with additional fixtures that put light down on cabinets, floor, and wall surfaces. Use accent lights, downlights, and/or portable fixtures.

Several wall-mounted fixtures of the same style create a rhythm in the space. It is unifying. Never mix styles of wall-mounted fixtures in the same room. In general, do not use translucent-shaded wall fixtures on a dark wall. Too much contrast is created. Do use opaque shades on up and down fixtures, forcing the light to the wall and ceiling surfaces.

Likewise, several pendants in the same style create a rhythm and are unifying. The repetition is pleasing when the fixtures are not overly ornate. Ribbed, prismatic-glass pendants look good repeated and blend with most furniture styles. Use the pendants in a row. They are successful when used over large kitchen islands, vanity tops, counters, or other long table-height cabinets.

SIZES OF DECORATIVE FIXTURES

How wide should a decorative fixture be? How high should it be hung? The answers to these questions depend upon many pieces of information, including whether hung over a table or in the center of a room, height of the ceiling, and the appearance of the fixture itself. Over kitchen tables or kitchen and bath countertops, chandeliers and pendants need to be 12 inches smaller in width than the width of the table or countertop. Some designers choose a chandelier one-half the width of the top. Further, in 8-foot ceilings, chandeliers and pendants can be hung 30 inches above the table or countertop. For higher ceilings, hang 3 inches higher for each additional foot of ceiling height. Consequently, a 10-foot high ceiling would have a chandelier hung 36 inches above the table or countertop.

Hung in the center of a room, chandeliers and pendants can be in inches what the diameter of the room is in feet. Some designers double the narrowest dimension (length or width) of the room and translate it to inches for the fixture width.

The appearance of the fixture further refines these guidelines. In general, delicate chandeliers with many arms appear smaller than they really are. Opaque solid pendants appear larger than they really are. Go bigger or smaller as necessary due to the style of the fixture and the room size.

A chandelier should be 2'-6" above the table.

A chandelier can be 12" smaller than the diameter of the table.

In kitchens and baths with high ceilings (above 8 feet), use two- or three-tiered chandeliers. They soar into the height, flattering the architecture. Single-tiered chandeliers look tiny in spaces with two- or three-story ceilings. It might be necessary to have the factory wire the chandelier with additional chain or cord prior to shipping so the fixture can hang within view. Chain- and cord-hung chandeliers or pendants adapt well to sloped high ceilings, whereas most rod-hung fixtures do not.

LAMPS FOR DECORATIVE FIXTURES

Do not demand that decorative fixtures light the whole room. In fact, have them give soft light. Otherwise, glare is created. If you can see the lamps, use 15 watts or less for each lamp. Even consider purchasing a low-voltage chandelier or pendant or rewiring a line-voltage fixture to use low-voltage, low-wattage lamps. If you cannot see the lamps because they are shielded (with shades, globes, or other coverings), use 15 watts or more as needed. However, never exceed the manufacturer's recommendation of maximum watts. Following these rules will assure that the lighting is safe and easy on the eyes.

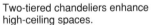

Two-tiered chandeliers enhance high-ceiling spaces.

A chandelier can measure in inches what the diagonal of the room measures in feet.

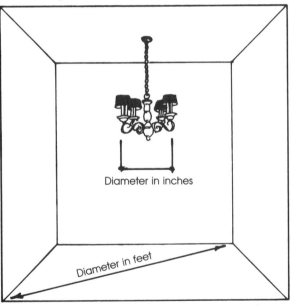

Diameter in inches

Diameter in feet

LIGHT DISTRIBUTION FROM DECORATIVE FIXTURES.

Direct.

Semi-direct.

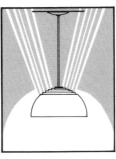

Direct-indirect.

General diffused.

Semi-indirect.

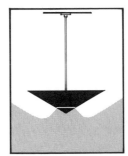

Indirect.

Rule of Thumb for Decorative Lamp Sizes

If lamp is visible, use 15 watts or less.

If lamp is hidden, use 15 watts or more, but not more than manufacturer specifies.

DECORATIVE FIXTURES FOR TASK LIGHT

Besides aesthetics, decorative fixtures can provide task light. All downlights in suitable positions provide task light. Consequently, pendants with downlight and chandeliers with built-in downlights can illuminate tasks. Whenever possible, choose such fixtures for over a table-height work surface. Likewise, wall fixtures suitably positioned can provide task light. Never have a wall fixture in front of and above a task. It will create a glaring reflection on glossy reading material. This glare is called a veiling reflection. Avoid it.

Portable fixtures are rarely used successfully for task light in kitchens, except at desks. Kitchen desks with computers are served best with adjustable portable fixtures.

Moreover, portable fixtures are rarely used successfully for task light in baths. However, for a real challenge, design a bathroom with only portable fixtures. The result is charming in historic-style residences but difficult to do.

Decorative low-voltage, bare-wire fixtures are portable and renters (or owners) can use them for both task and decorative effects, taking them along at moving time. The wires are suspended between walls and the high-tech fixtures are attached to the wires. The required transformer can be hidden in a cabinet. The size of the transformer limits the number of MR- or T-lamp fixtures usable. The wires do not give shocks and are the ultimate of movable, high-tech lighting.

PRICE JUSTIFICATION

After looking at the various options for decorative fixtures, you will wonder if the price can be justified. The answer is yes, if it is affordable. Purchase the most expensive fixture possible. Like jewelry, it is a once-in-a-lifetime investment. Stylish decorative fixtures give pleasure and increase the resale value of a residence. Don't miss out on their benefits. A decorative fixture will last for the life of a structure. That's a long time. Unlike bathroom faucets and kitchen countertops, lighting does not wear out from use, only from abuse. So, put as much as possible into it. It will pay back visually every day of the year. Compared to other interior furnishing, lighting is not costly. Further, it is one of the least expensive ways to decorate.

DECORATIVE-EFFECT FIXTURES

Fiber-optics that are end-lit and low-voltage sources in tubes, panels, and strings and on bare wires can create decorative effects.

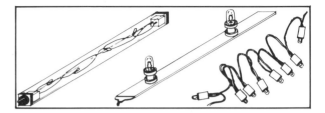

Low-voltage fixtures.

Decorative-Effect Fixtures
- end-lit fiber optics
- low-voltage tubes, panels, strings, and bare-wire strung

End-lit fiber optics can create multiple pin points of light in countertops, backsplashes, walls, and ceilings. A bar cabinet would be enhanced by such lights. The North Star Surfaces showroom in Minneapolis features it. The fibers are inserted in holes drilled in the countertop and then sanded smooth. A single MR lamp lights the many holes. A color filter or color wheel can change the color of the light, if desirable.

End-lit fiber optics brighten a countertop.

North Star Surfaces

Low-voltage tubes, panels, and strings can be decorative with tiny point sources gleaming brightly. The tubes lend themselves well to outline architecture, such as an etched-glass divider between a toilet and the rest of the bathroom, or the aperture of a shower skylight. (Be sure to specify waterproof for bathroom installations.) Further, tubes can be strung as a curtain between areas, making a transparent glittering screen. They also can be hung in varying lengths as a special chandelier.

Low-voltage panels can be ceiling or wall installed to create infinity or starlike patterns of gold or blue-white lamps in a field of deep bronze or blue, a never-tiring visual array. Try them at vanity dressing areas.

Low-voltage lamps on strings can be like fireflies in the branches of trees and other interior plants. Further, low-voltage strips can outline stemware racks inside or under upper cabinets in the kitchen or bar. They can also be installed as visible sources in any of the locations covered in *Low-Voltage Strips* in this chapter.

Low-voltage, bare-wire fixtures are MR or T lamps in lamp holders, much like miniature track fixtures. They are attached to shock-free wires usually stretched from wall to wall near the ceiling. They can be totally decorative and also provide light for tasks.

All low voltage begs for creative uses and never disappoints. The rows of visible lights have been used to attract and please the human eye. At low wattage they consume minimal energy and are cost effective.

Low-voltage tubes outline etched-glass divider.

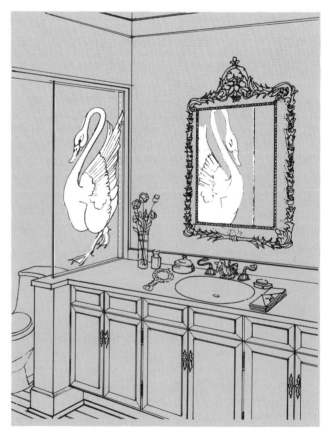

Phylrich, Int.

Decorative Fixture Vocabulary

Back Plate: a metal plate on a wall-mounted fixture that is attached to the wall. With permanently wired fixtures, it covers the electrical outlet box. With portable fixtures, it covers the hook. (The equivalent for hanging fixtures is a canopy.)

Billiard or Library Light: two or more pendants in a straight line on a stem from the ceiling.

Canopy: a metal plate that attaches the chain, stem, or cord of the chandelier or pendant to the ceiling. It covers the outlet box.

Chain: metal links that attach a chandelier or pendant to the ceiling.

Chandelier: a ceiling-mounted fixture with arms that hangs on a chain, stem, or cord.

Chandelier Arm: the extension out from the body of a chandelier to support the lights. (The main decorative elements of a chandelier.)

Channel: linear housing for low-voltage or linear lamps, either fluorescent or incandescent.

Chimney: glass that covers the light source and diffuses the light if frosted.

Crystal: clear glass of high brilliance and clarity used in drops, jewels, and festoons on the arms of a chandelier.

End-Lit Fiber Optics: Fibers that transmit light out the ends only.

Etched Glass: glass altered by acid, usually created in a pattern. It appears frosted.

Globe: glass enclosure for a light source. When opal or frosted, it diffuses the light.

Hard Wired Fixture: wired directly into the electrical system through a junction box.

Lead Crystal: quality glass with a higher brilliance.

Low-Voltage Panels: large plastic panels with low-voltage T lamps embedded inside.

Low-Voltage String: flexible wires with low-voltage S-lamp holders.

Low-Voltage Tape: flexible or rigid tape with low-voltage T- or S-lamp holders.

Low-Voltage Tubes: flexible or rigid plastic tubing with low-voltage T lamps inside.

Low-Voltage Wire Strung: low-voltage lamp holders strung on wires below the ceiling between walls.

Opal Glass: milky-white glass that diffuses well.

Outlet-Box Mount: permanently wired wall fixture.

Pendant: a ceiling-mounted fixture that hangs on a chain, stem, or cord with a shade, translucent or opaque, covering the light source.

Pinup: wall fixture with cord and plug.

Porcelain Socket: a ceramic keyless lamp holder for hidden installations.

Portable Fixture: table, wall, or floor fixtures that plug into a wall receptacle.

Prismatic Glass: a translucent shade of glass formed in ridges made by the prisms.

Scroll: decorative metal in S, C, or J shapes on chandeliers and pendants.

Shade: opaque or translucent covering, shielding the light source.

Stem: a rigid tube that suspends a pendant or chandelier from the ceiling.

Tiers: rows of chandelier arms arranged one above another.

Wall-Mounted Fixture: a portable or hard-wired fixture that hangs on the wall yielding up-, and/or downlight, or general light.

Wall-mounted.   Pinup.

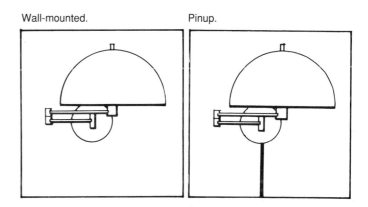

When purchasing a decorative fixture, knowing the terminology helps. Unfortunately, the terms are not consistent. For example, one manufacturer calls a portable wall fixture a "cord-and-plug mount." Another calls it a "pinup." A hard-wired fixture is called an "outlet-box mounted" by one and a "wall-mount" by another. Consequently, be attuned to synonyms of the terms you might hear.

Overall, fixtures for kitchens and baths are almost infinite. The choices should be well considered to get the most desirable results for both kitchens and baths.

chapter

6

electrical service

In our present technology, electricity supplies artificial lighting. However, fiber-optic technology can gather and bring sunlight to interior spaces in the daytime. But the expense of collecting and storing it for nighttime is not yet low enough to make it viable. As our technology advances, superconductivity at room temperature might be possible. Similarly, nuclear fusion, the clean nuclear power, is possible, but will take years to be available for commercial use. Such developments will change our dependence upon unrenewable resources. But until that time, choose the most energy-efficient lamps possible.

Making electricity consumes precious unrenewable resources (coal, gas, and oil) or generates toxic waste with a fatal risk (nuclear fission). Consequently, conserve energy by installing the most energy-efficient lighting possible. Frequently, old prejudices and cheap initial costs are the deciding factors, resulting in energy-inefficient choices that continue inefficiency for years. Do not do it! Higher initial costs are quickly paid back in energy-saving costs and continue as savings forever.

Lighting design is different than the design of electrical service. Lighting can be designed without knowing a lot about electricity. However, familiarity with electrical terms and concepts is helpful. Compare electrical service to a water supply system. The generator at the electric power company is like the pumping station at the water reservoir, and the transmission lines are like the water pipes under the street. The generator creates voltage to push the electricity into the transmission lines. Inside a residence, the electricity is supplied by "hot" wires. Wall receptacles or light fixtures are at various points along the wires. Wall switches are like the faucet. When the switch is turned on, the electricity flows. Then, like water, the electricity drains back, completing the circuit. A difference is that the electricity has an additional drain—a ground wire, protecting against excess current which could cause shocks and fire.

An incandescent lamp lights by creating resistance to the voltage in the filament, becoming hot and glowing. A fluorescent lamp lights by electrons causing the phosphors inside the tube to glow. Turning off and on

Electricity delivery compared
to water delivery.

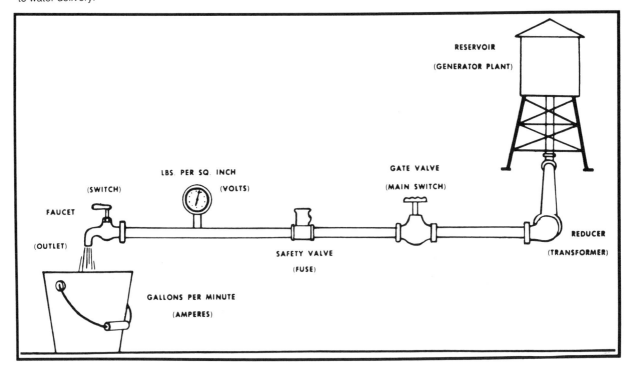

RESERVOIR

(GENERATOR PLANT)

LBS. PER SQ. INCH

(SWITCH) (VOLTS)

FAUCET

(OUTLET)

GATE VALVE

(MAIN SWITCH)

REDUCER

(TRANSFORMER)

SAFETY VALVE

(FUSE)

GALLONS PER MINUTE

(AMPERES)

Florida Power

frequently does not hurt the incandescent filament, but does hurt the fluorescent phosphors.

Volt is the measure of electrical pressure. Typically, residential voltage is 120 for lighting and 240 for ovens, ranges, and clothes dryers. However, the volts can vary as much as plus or minus 6 at any time. (Commercial structures usually have 240 for lighting.) Voltage is lost as the current moves through the fixture it supplies.

Ampere is the number of electrons that flow past. Amps are never lost, and they can kill. Watts are the rate at which the lamp consumes electricity.

The Relationship of Volts, Amps, and Watts

Volts x Amps = Watts
Watts ÷ Volts = Amps

For example, if the volts are 120 and the appliance requires 4 amps, the wattage used will be 480. Or turned around, if the appliance requires 1,200 watts and the volts are 120, then 10 amps will be needed.

Kilowatt-hour (Kwh) is the basic billing unit. It can be 1,000 watts for 1 hour or 1 watt for 1,000 hours. Operating costs can be calculated from it.

How to Calculate Electricity Costs

$$\frac{\text{Watts x Hours Used x Days}}{1,000} \times \text{Cost Kwh} = \text{Cost}$$

Average Kwh costs are 10 cents. Lighting design systems can be evaluated and compared with this formula.

Electrical current is in the form of electrons, not molecules of hydrogen and oxygen, like water. In this country, it is alternating current. (Batteries are direct current.) Electricity is carried by wires that are different sizes according to the load they carry, rated in amperes. Total amperage must not exceed the capacity of the circuit. For example, a track for track lighting must not be overloaded with more amperage than it or its circuit can carry. Similarly, a programmable dimmer is also rated. Consequently, adhere to total wattage allowable for these electrical devices.

Electrical codes regulate wire size. Line-voltage wires are black for the hot wire, white for neutral, and bare for ground wire. The wire bundles are insulated, either waterproof or not waterproof. Some are encased in steel or conduits for greater protection.

Built-in fixtures are hard wired. On the one hand, wires for built-in, line-voltage fixtures (recessed, wall-mount, etc.) must be joined at an electrical junction box. On the other hand, wires for low-voltage fixtures can be joined directly to the fixture. In fact, low-voltage fixtures can be safely strung on bare wires within the room. The wires can be touched with no shock. They are an effective attention getter.

Portable fixtures are wired through a cord and plug, and are connected to the electricity at a wall receptacle, like any electrical appliance. Manufacturers call them either outlet-box mount or cord and plug, even though they are the same. A baseboard wall receptacle is less in view at 10 inches above the floor. However, 15 is usually a code requirement. The American Disabilities Act indicates that a wheelchair user can only reach forward from the chair to 15, but they could reach to 10 inches from the side.

Electricity is hazardous. It can create fatal shocks with as little as one tenth of an amp (one half of the current required to light a 25-watt lamp) and can cause fires. Safety is critical in electrical installations. Hire only trained and licensed electricians. Purchase only Underwriters Laboratories (UL) listed fixtures. Safety first and foremost!

Wall receptacle.

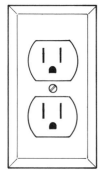

Ground fault interrupter.

Protective Electric Devices

In residences, circuit breakers protect against major excess electrical current. In addition, a ground fault interrupter (GFI) is a protective device that shuts off the flow of electricity at the slightest change in current too small to be detected by the circuit breaker. The GFI

prevents electric shocks, sometimes fatal, from electrical appliances. They are required by the National Electric Code for all new construction on kitchen and bath circuits with wall receptacles within 6 feet of water. Also, they should be specified for remodeling (and for your own residence). The GFI electronically compares the amperage flowing in one wire with the amperage flowing out the other. If they are equal, all is well. If they are not equal (even .005 amps difference), it shuts off the electricity. The GFI can be installed at a receptacle or at the circuit breaker. At the receptacle, it protects the other receptacles on the circuit ahead of it—none behind. Hence, if the receptacle is first on the circuit, all others will be protected. If last, no others will be protected. At the circuit breaker, the whole circuit benefits. Instruct your client to test the GFI every month. They are an inexpensive and powerful safety device. Use them!

Types of Service

LINE VOLTAGE

Line-voltage service is 120 volts for lighting kitchens and baths. All junction boxes for hard-wired fixtures and all receptacles for plugging in portable fixtures are 120 volts. Line-voltage service requires well-insulated 12- and 14-gauge wires. It is easy for new construction, but more difficult for remodeling.

All discharge-lamp fixtures—fluorescent, cold cathode, sodium, and neon—require a ballast or a transformer to match the electrical current with the requirements of the lamp. If the transformer needs to increase the current, it is called a step-up transformer.

Ballasts

Fluorescent lamps require ballasts. Since ballasts must be compatible with the lamp, they are often classified by the lamp-starting characteristics. Two different types of fluorescent ballasts are made. They are magnetic (core

Ballast.

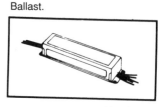

Metalux

and coil or reactance) and electronic (solid state). The core-and-coil ballasts are used for rapid-start and for instant-start fluorescent lamps. Some save energy, operate cooler, and last longer. Reactance ballasts are used for low-wattage, preheated fluorescent sources, but require an external starter.

The second type of ballast, electronic, is also called solid state. Electronic ballasts are used for fluorescent. They operate the lamp at a high frequency, increasing source efficacy and eliminating the fluorescent flicker that bothers some people. However, the frequency is in the radio frequency range and can affect any electronic equipment. Consequently, the Federal Communication Commission requires a radio-frequency interference (RFI) device. Electronic ballasts are more delicate than magnetic ballasts. They can be damaged by electrical surges, but some manufacturers build in transient surge protection.

Energy consumption for ballasts differ. On the one hand, a two-lamp, 40-watt fluorescent fixture and core-and-coil ballast consumes 16 watts for a total of 96 watts, including the lamps. On the other hand, electronic ballasts cut the wattage. They do the job for a total of 70 watts (15 for the ballast and 55 for the two lamps). (Lamp watts are reduced by a cooler ballast and cooler operating lamps, translating into less total watts consumed.) The reactance ballast consumes 18 watts and demands 80 for the two lamps for a total of 98.

Electricity Used by Fluorescent Ballasts Using Two 40-Watt Lamps

BALLAST TYPE	SOURCE WATTS	BALLAST WATTS	TOTAL WATTS USED
Core & coil	80	16	96
Electronic	55	15	70
Reactance	80	18	98

General Electric

Ballasts have little tolerance for variability. They are adversely affected by temperature and by wrong lamps. Many ballasts are thermally protected against internally overheating (indicated by a class P). A thermal protector that turns off the ballast if it overheats is required by the National Electric Code. Ballasts are designed to start lamps at certain minimum temperatures. Most are designed for 50° starting. Ballasts are sound rated, A to

D, indicating quietness. A is the quietest. Ballast hum is a symphony most people do not want to hear.

Standards for ballasts are set by the American National Standards Institute (ANSI), and a CBM label (Certified Ballast Manufacturer) indicates that they meet ANSI specifications. A UL label (Underwriters Laboratories) indicates that the United States safety criteria standards are met (CSA for Canada).

Labels indicate information about ballast standards. Labels show voltage and line-current requirements. Labels show approval for meeting thermal-protection requirements—class P. Labels show "no PCB," if no carcinogenic polychlorinated biphenyl is used. Labels show type of light sources UL listed for the ballast. Labels show HPF (high-power factor), indicating that the ballast delivers more energy and consumes less. (Many states have codes requiring the HPF ballasts. Some utility companies charge a penalty for installations using low-power factor ballasts, thereby causing a greater and unnecessary electricity demand.) Ballasts have standards of performance; choose the best.

LOW VOLTAGE

Low-voltage service is delivered to the transformer at 120 volts, and the transformer reduces voltage to the amount needed (usually 24, 12, or 6). Low-voltage strip lights, for example, require 12 or 24 volts, not 120, as delivered. Consequently, a step-down transformer is needed. Transformers are rated by the volt times amps (VA) that they can accommodate. Consequently, do not over watt a transformer. Determine the wattage needed for lighting, add twenty percent for current variability, and purchase a transformer capable of carrying the load. Typical sizes are 50, 100, 150, and 250 watts.

Transformer.

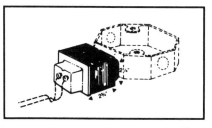

NeoRay

Rule of Thumb for Capacity of Low-Voltage Transformers

Total watts for lights + 20% for overload protection = wattage demand

Wattage demand = volts x amps of transformer (or VA rating)

For example, a 250 VA-rated transformer can manage 200 watts either at 4 fixtures of 50 watts each or 8 fixtures of 25 watts each.

A fuse should be installed between the transformer and the low-voltage lamps. Choose a Class II or UL approved transformer. Further, if dimming is critical, dim on the line-voltage side of the transformer with a low-voltage dimmer. Dimming should not be necessary, since low voltage is usually soft lighting anyway.

How a dimmer works.

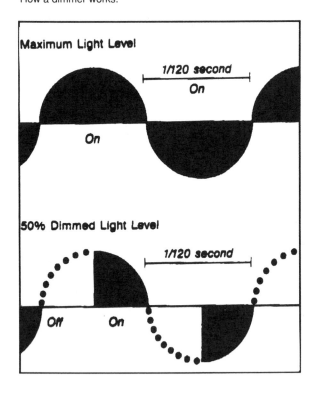

Maximum Light Level

1/120 second
On

On

50% Dimmed Light Level

1/120 second

Off   On

Lutron

Low-voltage service requires smaller wires, often in 16 and 18 gauge, which can be easily installed for remodeling and do not require electrical junction-box connections after the transformer and no ground wire. In fact, low-voltage service does not give fatal shocks, and the fire hazard is reduced. But because the wires are small, the current is quickly lost along the wires.

Consequently, install the transformer as close to the light sources as possible.

Voltage Drop Table

Wire Gauge	Maximum Number of Feet in Run to Keep Voltage Drop Under 5%								
14	72	36	27	23	17	13	10	8	6
12	108	54	42	38	29	21	18	14	10
10	174	87	67	58	45	34	28	22	17
8	278	139	108	92	72	54	45	36	27
6	442	221	172	146	114	86	72	57	43
Total Watts on Run	20	40	50	60	75	100	125	150	200

Capri

Electricity drops as it travels along the wires and what might start out as 12 volts can arrive as 10 or less, reducing brightness. Keep voltage drop to 5 percent. Locate transformers as close to sources as possible in a well-ventilated, accessible place.

Switching

A switch controls all hard-wired fixtures. If only one place is required to control the fixture, a single-pole wall switch or pull chain is used. If two places are required, 2 three-way wall switches are used (not a double-pole switch). If three or more places are required, four-way switches are used.

Portable fixtures are controlled by a switch on the fixture or the cord. Some contain dimmers. A wall switch can override a fixture switch, as long as the wall outlet for the fixture is wired into a wall switch.

Height of switches look best at 43 inches on center above the finished floor. They are comfortably low in the line of sight. Switches for wheelchair users work well at the same height on both unobstructed walls and walls behind countertops. The American Disabilities Act (ADA) requires in new construction and remodeling that switches be no higher than 54 inches for side approaches of the wheelchair and no higher than 48 inches for front approaches at unobstructed walls. Further, the Act indicates that the wheelchair user can typically reach no higher than 44 inches if the obstruction is a shelf-hung (open below) countertop of standard 24-inch depth. With shelf-hung countertops of 20 inches or less, the reach can be as high as 48 inches. Consult the Federal Register for ADA requirements and confer with local and state code requirements that might be more stringent.

High forward reach.

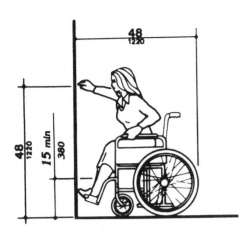

Maximum forward reach over obstruction.

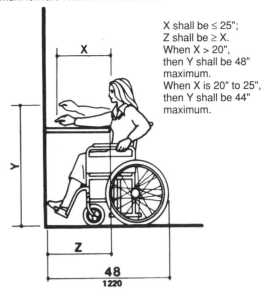

X shall be ≤ 25";
Z shall be ≥ X.
When X > 20",
then Y shall be 48"
maximum.
When X is 20" to 25",
then Y shall be 44"
maximum.

High and low side reaches.

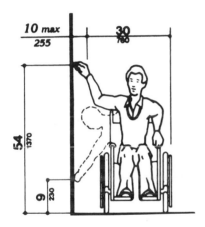

Maximum side reach over obstruction.

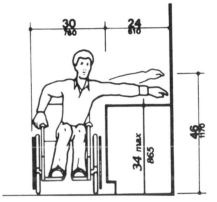

Federal Register

Dimmers

Dimmers have the power to create atmosphere in kitchens and baths. Dimmers can fine-tune a well-orchestrated lighting design. They can change lighting emphasis. They can tone up or tone down the total lighting at a slow rate that is almost unnoticed by the people using the space. Toning down saves lamp life, if lamps are line-voltage incandescent, and saves some electricity.

How does a dimmer work? An electronic (or solid-state) dimmer is basically a switch. It dims lights by turning the power on and off 120 times a second. Dimming occurs by controlling the amount of time the power is on versus off. The longer the power is off, the more light dims. When off, some energy is saved, but the color of the light may change.

Incandescent light gets more orange. Fluorescent light does not change, but may be too dull, if it is the only source of light.

Dimmers can be knobs or slides. Some slide dimmers allow limiting the range of dimming, thereby adding another dimension of control.

Basically, every light source is dimmable, but some sources cannot be dimmed to dark. Some last longer if dimmed. In general, all incandescent can be totally dimmed and last longer if they are. Fluorescent cannot be dimmed to dark and does not last any longer. Cold cathode and neon cannot be totally dimmed, do not last longer, and change color, depending upon their original color. (Experiment with them before specifying.)

Different light sources require special dimmers and dimmable ballasts. Low-voltage incandescent needs low-voltage dimmers. Low voltage must be dimmed on the line-voltage side. Autotransformers dim low voltage, but they are large and do not integrate well with complex dimming systems. For the most part, fluorescent and cold cathode require solid-state electronics for dimming. Solid-state dimmers reduce the flicker of fluorescent lamps that bother some people. Line-voltage incandescent is the easiest to dim.

Dimming higher-wattage, line-voltage incandescent lamps can lengthen their life. This advantage is useful in high-ceiling spaces where lamp replacements are difficult and light from the ceiling is required. Install a higher wattage incandescent than needed and dim with a slide dimmer set to limit the brightness. Lamp replacements will be less frequent.

Unfortunately, dimming can create noise. Line-voltage incandescent may buzz. To decrease the buzz, use lamps with less wattage, a smaller size, or a rough-service type. If all else fails, get debuzzing coils. Never use a lighting dimmer to control a fan, but a fan control can dim incandescent sources. When using a PAR and an electronic dimmer, the dimmer needs a debuzzing coil. When dimmed, fluorescent ballasts can hum and can vibrate if ballasts are poorly attached to the fixtures. Solve the problem by purchasing an A-rated or solid-state ballast. If not, install the ballast remotely. In addition, dimming can cause flickering at the ends of the fluorescent lamp. Solve by only using a dimmer designed for the fluorescent source and by not dimming energy-saving fluorescent. Solid-state ballasts cure both noise and flicker problems. Do not mix a solid-state transformer and a solid-state dimmer, unless the dimmer is specifically designed for such a transformer.

If low-voltage halogen sources are dimmed and the lamp appears to darken, operate at full power for 10 minutes in order to allow the tungsten cycle to regenerate. (Darkening does not affect the life of the lamp.) Do not operate dimmed low-voltage circuits without all the light sources in place and replace burned out sources promptly. Some low-voltage fixtures cannot be dimmed; check manufacturers' catalogs.

In general, dimmers were designed to dim, not to save electricity. Dimmers consume electricity themselves, even when off. The smallest dimmer consumes about ½ watt. Dimmers are not totally efficient. They spend 2 percent of their electricity producing heat. This heat is dissipated around the dimmer. Some newly engineered dimmers do not require a large electrical box to get rid of the heat. They are cool, slim, and trim. Some can be controlled remotely, a convenience for quick changes or for the executive-type personality, the ill, and the handicapped.

Hire the best qualified electrician and assure yourself of getting the best electrical service design and installation of fixtures.

chapter

7

lighting kitchens
with electric light

Kitchens are small (less than 168 square feet), medium (up to 250), or large (over 250). Whatever the size, they are the most expensive space in a residence, and the costs vary. Some are as little as eight thousand dollars and others are as much as forty-seven thousand. The average is around twenty, according to a recent survey by the University of Minnesota. Overall, standard appliances in any kitchen cost at least three thousand dollars. Lighting usually does not. Lighting should be at least four percent of the kitchen cost. If the design is done thoughtfully and choices are wise, the more spent on lighting, the better the lighting will be. Invest in good lighting; if energy efficient, it will pay back over the years.

In addition, the survey identified that clients feel that the type and location of lighting was almost as important as overall kitchen appearance/arrangement and location/amount of countertops. Let's give more than lip service to good lighting. Buy it!

Typically, kitchens have upper and lower cabinets fitted along one or more walls with continuous countertops and possibly a peninsula or island. Upper cabinets can go all the way to the ceiling or not. Such kitchens have many places to hide task and general lighting, and look suitable with many visible fixtures.

In contrast, country kitchens have an assembly of furniture—pie safes, sideboards, trestle tables, spice cupboards, dry sinks, and step-back hutches—as cabinets and countertops. They can be Shaker or other period style. Such kitchens are called unfitted. These kitchens are usually large with walls at least 15 feet long to accommodate placing furniture with space between. Unfitted kitchens offer few places to hide lighting and require skilled design to have unobtrusive lighting maintaining an understated appearance. Sometimes however, such kitchens have exposed structural elements—beams, pipes, and rafters—which could shield ceiling fixtures for general illumination. General illumination is difficult, because such kitchens are large. Also, lighting inside upper cupboards in furniture is hard. A center-ceiling chandelier does not

Fitted kitchen.

Unfitted kitchen.

do it well. Sometimes, unfitted kitchens have heavy cornice moldings suitable for hiding low-voltage strips. Much of the unobtrusive task lighting in this chapter can be furniture integrated, unless the furniture is a valuable antique and cannot be altered.

In fitted or unfitted kitchens, people who like to cook need more surfaces lighted than do people who do not cook. Nonetheless, noncooks need minimal lighting at the work counter, sink, cooking, and eating surfaces. Most kitchens have only a center-ceiling light, which is unsatisfactory. With a center-ceiling fixture, kitchen counters are in shadow wherever the person stands. Effective kitchen lighting illuminates the work surface, not the center of the room. Light at work surfaces reinforces the intended use of the location and focuses attention. Light the kitchen by first determining the surfaces to receive light and by identifying what lamp can provide the needed amount. Next, determine what fixture could hold the lamp and where it can be installed.

Fixtures for noncooks are usually less numerous; fixtures for cooks are more numerous and provide comfortable, well-integrated lighting. Some cooks may want to choose fixtures listed for noncooks for their own reasons. After determining locations, de-

termine the amount of light needed from each fixture. The amount required varies according to the color of kitchen surfaces, other sources available, including daylight, and condition of the user's eyes. The best method of determining how much light is needed is to test it. Often, people do not know how much light they require.

Both cooks and noncooks need a protected wall receptacle in the kitchen within 6 feet of water, as required by the National Electric Code. A ground fault interrupter will satisfy this requirement. It can provide protection against electrical shocks from small appliances. It can be installed at the receptacle or at the circuit-breaker panel. (See *Protective Electric Devices* in Chapter 6.)

See for Yourself #8: How Much Light Is Needed? Considering Fluorescent Light?

1. Determine the length of the linear or compact lamps that fit.
2. Take an incandescent lamp that is at least three but not more than four times the wattage of the fluorescent lamp. (For example, to test light from a 40-watt fluorescent, hold up a 150-watt incandescent lamp.)
3. Hold the incandescent where you would install the fluorescent.
4. Observe whether the light delivered is sufficient; do not look at the lamp itself or the size

of the area lighted, just the amount of light. If it is not sufficient, choose a fixture that has two fluorescent lamps in it.

Considering incandescent light?
1. Identify the amount of wattage the manufacturer specifies for the fixture under consideration.
2. Take an incandescent lamp of that wattage and hold it where the fixture would be installed.
3. Observe whether the amount of light delivered is sufficient. If not, add more light by choosing a fixture that can deliver more, or choose additional fixtures for other locations.

task surfaces

At the Countertop

To illuminate work locations in fitted kitchens at a countertop, fixtures can be hung under the upper cabinets, on the ceiling, or between upper cabinets. To illuminate work locations in unfitted kitchens, fixtures can be hung under the upper cupboards in tall furniture, be on the ceiling, or hidden in a canopy holding pots and pans. Noncooks will probably have only one counter to light; cooks will probably have several. Overall, the popularity of countertop lighting has increased threefold, according to a National Kitchen and Bath report. It should; it is the most important surface to light.

CABINET ABOVE THE COUNTERTOP

Attach a fixture to an upper cabinet above the countertop whenever possible. Fluorescent is excellent—bright light and little heat; but low-voltage tube or tape incandescent is suitable.

If using fluorescent, the choices are either linear or compact lamps. If choosing a linear, use one that is two-thirds the length of the counter. If choosing compacts, use closely spaced, single-bent tubes in 7 or 9 watts on a metal channel for the full length of the countertop.

For renters, a portable, fluorescent throwaway fixture or a low-voltage, linear strip with a built-in transformer are ideal. Both have plugs and switches. For owners, install ready-made or custom-made fluorescent fixtures permanently into a junction box behind the wall. Ready-made fixtures usually utilize mini-bipin fluorescent. Some fixtures hide the source; some do not. A miniature, shielded track holds a fluorescent lamp (as well as line-voltage incandescent). A custom-made installation consists of a fluorescent medium bipin tube, either a 1-inch diameter T8 or a 1½-inch T12 and a holder (channel). All should be located at the front edge of the upper cabinet for the best light distribution and be well hidden from view. Install at the back only if the backsplash is a matte finish. A glossy backsplash reflects like a mirror any sources hung on upper cabinets.

Glare can be omitted by furred cabinets standing off the wall with lighting above and below. Use cabinets that do not go all the way to the ceiling and attach two 2-by-4-inch strips mounted on the wall 4 inches from the top and the bottom of the cabinet. Mount the fixtures on the furring, giving uplight to the ceiling and downlight to the countertop.

Furred-out cabinets.

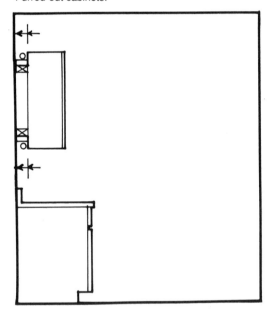

Remember that lights are viewed from several positions in a kitchen—standing and seated, even from another room. Consequently, even though under the upper cabinets, the fixtures need shielding. A portable fluorescent fixture can be installed to be its own shield. A ready-made track has shielding. Upper cabinets themselves can provide shielding, particularly custom-made cabinets.

A door can hide the fixture.

A recessed shelf holds a fluorescent light.

Upper-Cabinet Shielding

■ a door that hangs below the bottom shelf.
■ cabinet recess.
■ a recess in the back half of the lower shelf creates a place for the channel. (Inside the cabinet, the recessed shelf creates storage for short objects—canned goods, glasses, and cups.)
■ a recess at the wall created by a furred-out cabinet.

Likewise, remember that the backsplash is lighted by under-cabinet fixtures. Typically, backsplashes cover the gap between the countertop and the bottom of upper cabinet. If backsplashes are glossy—glazed ceramic tile or high-gloss plastic laminate—they reflect any light sources. Low-voltage sources reflect as dots. Linear sources reflect as lines of light. Shield or recess them to avoid the reflection. If shielding or recessing is not possible, opt for a line of light, rather than dots.

Custom-made cabinets are not always required. Some ready-made cabinets already have built-in fluorescent fixtures and others can incorporate them with minor modifications. However, modify them before hanging; afterward it is more difficult.

Fluorescent channels sometimes need a diffuser or louver. If so, the recess in the cabinet needs to be 3½ inches deep to hold a diffuser or a louver. A diffuser spreads the light and hides the source. It can be prismatic or opal. A louver controls light in case the lamp might be seen by someone seated. A louver can be an egg-crate grid or a parabolic wedge.

If using incandescent, use low-voltage fixtures the same length of the countertop. Low-voltage tubes are suitable and have lamps encased in round or square plastic. Tapes are

Some ready-made cabinets
have built-in fixtures.

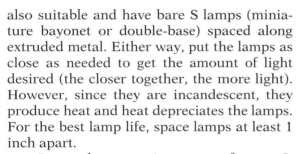

Low-voltage lamps reflect dots.

Linear lamps reflect a line.

also suitable and have bare S lamps (miniature bayonet or double-base) spaced along extruded metal. Either way, put the lamps as close as needed to get the amount of light desired (the closer together, the more light). However, since they are incandescent, they produce heat and heat depreciates the lamps. For the best lamp life, space lamps at least 1 inch apart.

Low voltage requires a transformer. It can be remotely mounted on top of or inside a cabinet, or elsewhere. It should be accessible; some codes require it. Low-voltage wires are small and easy to hide, good for both remodeling and new installations. The lamps burn out and should be easy to replace. Some strips have swivel sockets for convenience. (Get extra lamps since they are not always easy to find.) Some tubes have to be sent back to the factory for replacement. Some have an optional shield. All need shielding. Some must be cut by the factory. Others can be cut on the job. Lamps are available in ¼ to 5 watts. Like fluorescent, install low voltage at the front of the upper cabinets when possible.

NO CABINET ABOVE THE COUNTERTOP

When there is no cabinet above countertop,

illumination can come from a recessed, surface-mounted, or suspended ceiling fixture. Recessed is least obtrusive. Choose a ready-made fixture with a lens or diffuser. A lens either spreads or concentrates light; a diffuser scatters light and obscures the lamp. A dropped diffuser spreads more light than a flat one. Do not use an open ceiling fixture— a downlight with no diffuser or lens—unless extra brilliance is required. An open fixture gets dirty quickly and can be harsh, if it is used alone. Ceiling fixtures are far away from the surfaces that need light and, therefore, require more punch to get the light down. Use at least 40 fluorescent watts, around 75 incandescent line-voltage watts, or 50 low-voltage spot beam, according to individual needs.

Likewise, if the countertop is an island, a luminous panel in or on the ceiling, or a recessed cove can reinforce the architecture of the island. (See *Luminous Panel* in Chapter 5 and *Luminous Ceiling Installation* in Chapter 8.)

Also, illumination can come from a ready-made pendant or suspended fixture. The fixture can be functional or decorative. If decorative, it can provide a repeatable interior design feature when coordinated with the same fixture elsewhere in the room. Hang a

A repeatable decorative fixture.

pendant high enough to allow for headroom, but low enough not to see the source. Choose one that transmits light through the shade as well as down. Otherwise, light might be too harsh if it is the only source.

Finally, if there are upper cabinets to the left and right, illumination can come from either a lighted shelf or a lighted cornice stretched between them. The shelf holds the fixture and kitchen items. Light can go up and down, spreading over more than just the countertop. Three benefits are received from one shelf. The shelf can be made of wood, glass, or plastic. Use a fluorescent channel as wide as the shelf. Mount it under the front edge. If possible, use a rapid-start 36- or 48-inch fluorescent. It turns on instantly and, therefore, is the most suitable.

A lighted cornice can be either an opaque board with downlight or a leaded-glass panel lighting both through and down. (See *Luminous Panels* in Chapter 5.)

At the Sink

The most frequently used place in the kitchen is the sink. Even in an unfitted kitchen, the sink is a fixed location, and usually against a wall. In fitted or unfitted kitchens, light the

sink well. The amount should be enough to distinguish between a dirty and a clean dish. The fixture can be attached to the upper cabinet or to the ceiling. If there is a cornice board between two upper cabinets at the ceiling, a fixture can be mounted behind it.

MOUNTED BEHIND A CORNICE BOARD ON THE CEILING

If fluorescent is to be used, mount it behind a cornice board. The lamp should be as long as possible. For instance, if the width of the board is 50 inches, a 48-inch fluorescent channel would fit. The type of illumination produced is shadow free, but not very intense. The illumination from one fluorescent lamp might not be enough; two or three might be required.

If incandescent is to be used, a line-voltage or low-voltage MR in low wattage could give the punch of light required. The MR does the job while consuming less electricity and putting out less heat. For more watts, a line-voltage 75-watt R or ER is suitable. The ER puts out a medium-sized, intense area of light equivalent to the light from a 150-watt flood,

An opaque cornice board can hide a fixture.

St. Charles

but the ER is deeper than the R. Consequently, it must be installed in a deep fixture.

The fixtures could be a porcelain socket with a bare lamp, a downlight, recessed or surface mounted, or a track fixture with a canopy holder from the accessories in the track catalogs. If energy use is not a consideration, purchase a porcelain socket and an R line-voltage lamp, inexpensive and hidden from view.

If the cornice board is translucent (a leaded-glass panel), the light can provide both task and decorative illumination. (See *Luminous Panels* in this chapter.)

MOUNTED WITHOUT A CORNICE BOARD
ON THE CEILING

Use an open incandescent downlight if possible. It provides the most light. Either recessed or surface mounted, a downlight can hold line- or low-voltage MR at low wattage or a line-voltage R at 75 watts for a bright pool of light. Choose the lamp according to the intensity desired and beam width obtainable. Consult manufacturers' catalogs (particularly track or low-voltage fixture catalogs) for beam-spread charts. Measure the distance from ceiling to sink. Distances on charts are not always the exact distances needed. Thereupon, round the numbers and decide if more or less light is best—usually more, because surface colors absorb light and beam charts do not take color into consideration. Read the chart at the 0° aiming angle for the distance. Determine the footcandles expected. It should be at least 30 and can go up to 50 depending upon reflectance of surfaces receiving the light and age of user. (Dark surfaces and older age demand more light.) For example, a 20-watt MR16 would give 18 footcandles and a 42-watt MR16 would give 40. Err on the side of more rather than less at sinks, because lamps produce less light as they age, and surfaces get dirty and reflect less. Consequently, provide a little more at the beginning. Likewise, determine width of beam. It should be as wide as the sink.

If the upper cabinets do not go all the way to the ceiling (and if perchance the cabinets have panelled or other textured doors), drop the ceiling down to the top of and in front of the cabinets creating a dropped soffit. Install open incandescent downlights in the soffit in front of the upper cabinets and above the sink. The light will enhance the texture of the doors and provide excellent light at the sink and inside the upper cabinets. However, countertop lighting is still required, because the counter will be in shadow. (See *Dropped Soffits* in Chapter 5.)

If fluorescent is to be used, two compact fluorescent sources in a downlight or a double-lamp, linear fluorescent fixture, recessed or surface mounted, could be used. However, the light will not be as intense as incandescent, but it could be enough.

If a decorative statement is to be made or continued, a ceiling-hung pendant or two wall-hung uplights on either side of the sink could be used. A screw-based compact fluorescent source with a quiet electronic self-ballast could be installed in the pendant for energy-efficiency and the light, having less distance to travel, will be brighter than if originating from the ceiling. If uplights are the choice, make sure surfaces receiving light are pale in color to reflect as much as possible. Also, install uplights at least 10 inches down from the ceiling for good distribution.

At the Cooking Surface

Even noncooks need to see when water boils. Cooks need to see a lot more. Consequently, cooking surfaces (ranges, stove tops, or built-in units) need light. Unfitted kitchens are not likely to have a hood over the cooking surface, but fitted kitchens might. A lighted shelf over the range in an unfitted kitchen would be unobtrusive. In fitted or unfitted kitchens if a hood is used and has a light, lamp it with the wattage specified by the manufacturer. Do not reduce the wattage unless it creates a glare. A screw-based compact fluorescent source could be substituted if space permits and energy conservation is the goal. If a hood is not used, install a shielded fixture—shielded both from view and from splatter.

If upper cabinets are available, hang a well-shielded fluorescent fixture or build in an incandescent low-voltage or line-voltage fixture with a lens. Almost all low-voltage tube or tape lights are unsuitable to withstand the high temperatures of cooking surfaces.

If upper cabinets are not available, a lighted shelf, pendant, or ceiling fixture can illuminate the cooking surface. The amount and color of light is more critical for cooks who need to distinguish between opaque and translucent while stir-frying. Noncooks need

Lighted shelves.

to distinguish between browned and burned. But both cooks and noncooks will want at least 20 footcandles—usually the light provided from 30 fluorescent linear watts or 65- to 75-watt line-voltage incandescent. Use fluorescent whenever possible; it is cooler. The cooking surface produces enough heat. Infrared incandescent lamps or microwave ovens can keep food hot elsewhere. Save energy and minimize heat that could demand more air-conditioning.

At the Eating Surface

An eating surface may be a counter, bar, island, peninsula, or table. Noncooks are more likely to eat in the kitchen than are cooks. Eating surfaces that are not glossy look best with direct light. The more direct and intense it is, the more appealing the food looks. Incandescent produces the most direct and intense light.

OPEN DOWNLIGHTS

Direct and intense can come from any point-source fixture that puts light down hard on the eating surface—open downlights, either ceiling mounted, as a pendant, or in a chan-

delier. Downlight creates task light; the decorative lamps create general light. Many decorative shapes are available. (See *Lamps for Decorative Fixtures* in Chapter 4.) For the downlight, low-voltage, incandescent point sources (MR or PAR) give the greatest intensity for the lowest wattage. In line voltage, a PAR gives greater intensity at a lower wattage than R. But a well-engineered A-lamp downlight can give sufficient intensity. Check manufacturers' catalogs for data on fixtures with these sources. All enhance the look of food and tableware with sparkle, shadow, and vibrant color. Make every meal a visually appealing experience.

Downlight in a chandelier.

FRAMING PROJECTOR

The most distinctive and intense light for eating surfaces is produced by a framing projector. In theaters, it is used to precisely light stage objects. In eating areas, it can illuminate just the eating surface and nothing else. It is capable of cutting the edges of a light beam. When fully open, it can light an area about 60 by 60 inches. When closed down, it can light a smaller area. The light can be confined to shine brilliantly on all table settings and food, enhancing colors and appetites. The light source is a tungsten-halogen incandescent lamp. It requires careful handling, but burns brighter longer than other lamps. The fixture needs readjusting each time the lamp is replaced. These requirements are fine for some people and terrible for others.

The framing projector can be either recessed in the ceiling or track mounted. Thus, both owners and renters have equal opportunity for using this precise optical instrument.

If the eating surface is glossy—glass, polished marble, shiny plastic laminate, or lacquered wood—light it with reflected light. Otherwise, the glossy surface acts like a mirror reflecting any direct source of light as a spot of glare. The glare never goes away. Wall distributions (from brackets, cornices, perimeter troffers, soffits, and valances) are likely to be glare free. Uplight distributions (from wall sconces, pendants, coves, and canopies) can be glare free on the tabletop. A canopy has an advantage in that it can be directly over the eating surface and create a focal point.

CANOPY

Either a ready-made or custom-made canopy can be suspended over the eating surface. It can provide up and/or downlight. A ready-made canopy is stem mounted from the ceiling, is slick-looking, and complements any nontraditional interior. It requires linear fluorescent sources, but some permit adding incandescent accent fixtures.

Canopies can also be made of cloth.

A custom-made canopy can be a wooden frame, open above and covered with a diffuser or louver below. Linear fluorescent sources bounce light off the ceiling and down through the diffuser or louver. Incandescent accent fixtures can be included. Make the canopy within the sizes of fluorescent channels (2 to 8 feet). Suspend it 10 inches from the ceiling in an 8-foot ceiling and lower in a higher ceiling. Make the depth of the canopy at least 6 inches. The distance between the channels should be one and a half times the depth of the frame. The distance from a channel to the side of the frame should be half the distance between the channels. Therefore, if the frame is 6 inches deep, the channels should be 9 inches apart. Or a custom-made canopy can be a large, fire-retardant fabric shade hiding downlights. Make the canopy proportional to the eating surface, but narrower. (See *Canopies* in Chapter 5.)

At the Desk

Is work done at a kitchen desk? If so, eighty-five percent of the information is transmitted through the eyes. Therefore, lighting at a desk should maximize the ability to see information. Whether the desk is freestanding or part of the countertop, make the light the best possible. Whether the tasks are reading/writing or computer tasks, make the light the best possible.

Desk lighting to maximize the ability to see.

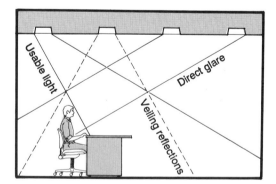

The best possible lighting is the best amount in the best position and best color to enhance vision. The amount required is influenced by many things, including age, readability, and length of time available and accuracy required for the task. Is the reading material glossy magazines or catalogs? Is it penciled longhand notes? Is it numbers that are small to input into a computer? Is it poor photocopies?

If these difficult visual tasks are being performed, more light is needed than if the tasks were sharp, simple, and unimportant. Sometimes, the best amount is as high as 200 footcandles (usually the amount supplied for architectural offices by ceiling-fluorescent troffers, if in the correct position). The best amount is not less than 30 footcandles (usually the amount in a reasonably lighted office).

For reading/writing tasks.

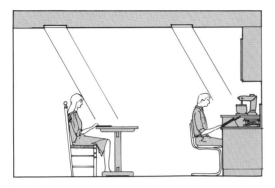

The best position depends upon the task. Both reading/writing and computer tasks require light that does not create reflected glare. The nonglare positions are the same for both tasks, if light comes from the left and/or right. The nonglare positions are opposites, if the light comes from above. For reading/writing tasks, ceiling or shelf fixtures need to be behind the person. For computer tasks, ceiling fixtures need to be in front. For both tasks, light should not only be on the task, but it should also be nearby in lesser amounts and farther away in lesser or greater amounts in order have the best possible light. The room must not be dark.

For computer tasks.

See for Yourself #9: Will There Be a Glare at the Desk?

1. Put a hand mirror on the desktop or hold where the computer screen would be.
2. See if a lighted source or brightly lighted surface is visible in the mirror.
3. If so, there will be glare.

The best color requires an understanding of the ability of the color of light to reveal contrast of black and white (the usual reading-matter colors). In general, cool colors of light (high in Kelvin degrees, 41°K) reveal contrast of reading matter the best; warm colors of light (incandescent and low Kelvin degree fluorescent, 30°K) do not. The triphosphor warm sources, 30° or 35°K reveal colors of the spectrum (red through violet) well. But unless color is part of the task, use cool white or 41°K at kitchen desks where reading and writing take place.

INTERIOR FINISHES

Interior finishes of the desk and other room surfaces influence the effectiveness of desk light. Never have a glossy desktop; glare would be unrelenting. Further, a heavily used desk should be pale in color to create a noncontrasting background to the task (white paper). Likewise, desks need nearby surfaces to be pale-colored with matte finishes. Beyond the desk, dark walls, floors, cabinets, or other major surfaces will reflect little light, possibly preventing the proper balance at the kitchen desk, especially if under lighted.

Rules of Thumb for Interior Finishes

- Never have a glossy finish on the desktop.
- Never put glass on top of a desk!
- A heavily used desk should be pale in color to create a noncontrasting background to the task (white paper).
- Countertop desks and desks next to the wall need pale-colored wall surfaces with a matte finish.
- Walls, floors, cabinets, or other major surfaces will reflect the light or not, depending upon their color. Design amount of light accordingly.

Light can actually hinder work. It can be too little or too much, can create a glare, or can be too contrasting. If any one of these conditions exist, the eyes and body strain and become fatigued. Specify both interior finishes and lighting carefully.

Wherever the fixture is located, the light should reflect away from the eyes. Light reflects from a surface at the same angle it falls on the surface, but in the opposite direction. Consequently, pay attention to the angle of light for reading/writing tasks.

Light should reflect away from, not in your eyes.

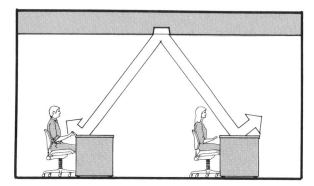

Portable Fixtures

A floor, table, or wall-mounted portable fixture used for desk light can be either adjustable or nonadjustable, but it must deliver light well over the desktop from a nonglare position. Whenever possible, purchase an adjustable fixture, giving greater range of positions. Whenever possible, use fluorescent sources; they are cool and energy efficient. If choosing incandescent, low-voltage fixtures are the smallest and can be the lowest wattage. Be aware that not all halogen fixtures are low voltage. Position a single desk fixture to avoid shadow—on the left side if right-handed, on the right if left-handed.

Adjustable fixture.

Translucent shade.

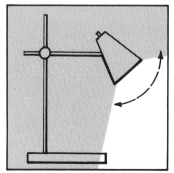
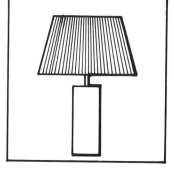

Portable Fixtures for Kitchen Desks

If fluorescent and:
- If using linear, never put it in front of the reading/writing task (parallel to the desktop). Position it perpendicular.
- If linear and positioned parallel, get a fixture with a batwing or bilateral ray lens to redistribute the light in two opposite directions.
- If using a pair of fixtures, put them perpendicular and on both sides, balancing the light.
- If using compact, get fixtures with reflectors.
- If using compact fixtures, allow space to hide the small ballast on the cord.
- If using fluorescent, specify an electronic ballast—very quiet.
- If long-term reading/writing tasks will take place, specify cool-white or 41°K linear, not compact. The color enhances black-and-white reading material.

If line-voltage incandescent:
- Use a three-way lamp to have variable light levels.
- Use a shade that transmits light.
- Have the bottom of the shade 16 inches wide.
- Have the bottom of the shade level with the eyes of the person seated.
- Use a glass bowl diffuser under the shade.
- Use a coated, never a clear, lamp.
- Have the ability to provide up to 200 watts.

If low-voltage incandescent:
- Use the lowest wattage possible to keep the desktop cool.
- Allow space to hide the small transformer on the cord.
- Get several lamp replacements because they may be hard to find.
- Handle halogen lamps with covered hands. Oils from fingers may cause the lamp to shatter.
- Choose a fixture with a lens if using open halogen lamps. Or choose a glass-enclosed lamp.

Sample Electric Cost

A 13-watt compact fluorescent saves $2.24 per month over a 200-watt incandescent when used for 4 hours per day at 10¢ per kilowatt-hour. And the fluorescent last longer than seven sets of incandescent lamps.

Ceiling Fixtures

Ceiling-hung pendants, chandeliers with downlights, and surface-mounted ceiling fixtures can also illuminate tables or desks. A single pendant, like a single fixture, needs to hang on the opposite side of the hand used for writing (or over the computer input). A pair of pendants could be on both sides. A linear pendant (a library light) can hang centered on the tabletop, illuminating from both sides. As a result, two different people using the same desk can be satisfied. The same satisfaction is obtainable with a pendant adapted to a ceiling track and moved from left to right as required.

Chandeliers with downlights can provide a sufficient amount of light, but the position could create glare on glossy reading material. A surface-mounted ceiling fixture with a lens is capable of spreading light. But position it above the head and never have a person's back to the light if it creates shadows. Avoid all open downlights; the light provided is harsh. If downlights have R or PAR lamps, radiant heat spills out. Use an A lamp, or better yet purchase a lens to soften the light. Lenses or louvers from the same manufacturer are often interchangeable with the same size aperture in other fixtures. Check manufacturers' catalogs.

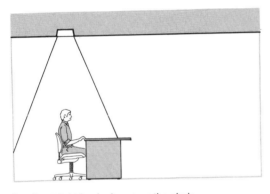

Put direct-light luminaires over the chair...

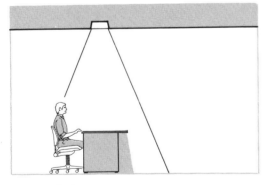

...not the desk.

Often a single ceiling fixture is used to illuminate a desk surface and the room. Not good!

The area around the desk needs no less than one-third as much light as the task. Further away, one-tenth as much is needed. As a result, light at the desk would not be surrounded by darkness and the eyes would not have to work hard. Consequently, three sources are needed for kitchen desk work, not one.

Under-Cabinet Fixtures and Lighted Shelves

Under-cabinet fixtures can provide excellent lighting. Manufacturers have carefully studied the problems of reflected glare from the under-cabinet position and have solved the problems in several ways. Some throw the light to the left and to the right with either a batwing lens, a reflector, or a louver. Others mount sources perpendicular to the wall and make them movable along a track for greater or lesser amounts of light. All have been innovative. All solve the same problem, but the end products are dissimilar. Choose the one that works for your installation. Do not choose ones that ignore lighting distribution problems.

Shelves with downlight (and/or uplight) are good, if they do not create reflected glare. Use fluorescent sources, particularly the compact, but avoid reflected glare. Either choose a fixture with a spread lens or side-lighting louvers, or mount the fluorescent sources perpendicular to the wall. Install the shelf 15 to 18 inches above the desktop and 9 to 12 inches back from the front edge of the desk.

COMPUTER TASKS

If a computer is used in the kitchen, the lighting problems are complex. Computer lighting and reading/writing lighting have diametrically opposed requirements. Eye fatigue from poor lighting is not limited to the office; it can happen at home.

The computer screen is glass and acts like a mirror reflecting any lighted surface (a shirt) or any visible lighted source (a ceiling fixture). The eyes must adjust to three values: the surroundings in view (vertical furniture surfaces, walls, and/or windows), the screen, and the hard copy for input. The values of these three surfaces might be different (dark or bright). If the eyes must adapt abruptly to different values, fatigue occurs. It is not only the chair that needs to be comfortable at the computer, but the eyes need to be also.

Surfaces

First, the computer user should not face a visible source (bare lamp or uncovered window) or a brightly lighted surface. The screen and its surroundings (a close or adjacent surface) should not have a luminance ratio of greater than 3:1. Otherwise, as the person looks up and down, his or her eyes must abruptly adjust and readjust. Likewise, the surroundings should be uniform in value. If a window is in view, it should be covered in a material that is the same color value as the wall. Surroundings should not distract the eyes from the task.

Monitor surroundings should be uniform in value.

Second, the screen should not face a visible source or a brightly lighted surface. Otherwise, reflection could obscure the information on the screen. A bright surface might be the top of the wall with cove lighting or might be a white shirt reflecting indirectly from a direct-light ceiling fixture. Keep all direct and indirect reflections off the screen.

Third, the surface surrounding the hardcopy input should not be exceedingly different in value. The amount of light selected for the hardcopy depends upon the age of the computer user, the speed and accuracy required, the contrast of the copy (typeface) and its background (paper), the luminance values of the copy and screen, and the angle of light. The older the worker, the more light needed. The poorer the contrast between copy and paper, the more light needed, unless the screen is a dark background. If so, the hardcopy input should not be overly bright. The eyes constantly try to adapt to brightness and darkness. The eyes get tired, producing a headache, neck and shoulder tension, or a

general sense of fatigue. If the screen is white or full color, the hardcopy input should be bright also. Screen brightness and copy brightness should be as equal as possible. Consider changing the screen background color. The contrast ratio of the task (screen's image and screen's background) should be 10:1.

Fourth, the amount of general illumination could be as low as 10 footcandles, but it should be between one-tenth to ten times as bright as the task.

Bad reflections.

Direct glare.

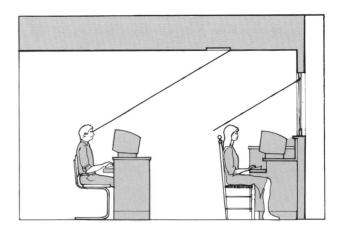

Fixtures

Both custom-made and ready-made fixtures can provide light in uplight or direct distributions. Uplight from coves, uplight brackets, and valances can give glare-free ceiling light. Fixtures providing uplight avoid the direct-angle glare problem, but can create too bright a surface that can reflect on the screen. Control the brightness and make it uniform. (See *Brackets, Canopies, Coves,* and *Valances* in Chapter 5.)

Rule of Thumb for Brightness Created by Uplights

Brightness should appear uniform. Hence, the ceiling surface should have a luminance ratio of 10:1 or less.

Direct light from perimeter troughs, dropped soffits, or brackets can be task light. They can deliver the glare-free angle with small-cell parabolic louvers or polarizing lenses depending upon their position. Ceiling-mounted fixtures should not distribute light above the 60° nor below the 30° angle (with 0° as straight down). (See *Brackets, Recessed Perimeter Troughs,* and *Soffits* in Chapter 5.)

Rule of Thumb for Glare-free Light from Ceiling Fixtures for Computers

Direct, above-the-head light should come from an angle between 30° and 60° up from vertical.

Under-cabinet or shelf fixtures should not create reflected glare on input material or create too bright a background for the screen. If the sources are at the left and right or have a special lens, reflected glare potential is minimized.

An uplight pendant can illuminate a countertop, peninsula, or freestanding desk with no upper cabinets. Use either linear fluorescent or incandescent sources.

Portable task fixtures can be used. Some clip on to hardcopy holders. Others are tabletop and adjustable. All should provide 20 to 30 footcandles. Likewise, the light should enhance black print on white paper. Black and white are enhanced by cool-white fluorescent. Compact fluorescent (9, 13, and 28 watts) gives a suitable amount of light, but the smaller wattage, even with reflectors, might not give enough light for long-term tasks. Further, their light is around 27°K—warmer than incandescent.

Both Tasks

The glare-free zone of direct light for reading/writing tasks is opposite to the glare-free zone for computer tasks. Consequently, if both tasks are required, separately switch to fixtures in each glare-free position. If ceiling mounted, one switch should control fixtures producing light suitable for reading/writing tasks and the second switch should control fixtures for the computer. Programmable dimmers can control these changes. They can be labeled for easy identification. (See *Programmable Dimmers*. Such dimmers are user friendly.) If portable fixtures are used, position them to provide glare-free light.

With indirect fixtures, both reading/writing and computer tasks can be suitably lighted, if the ceiling is uniform and not overly bright.

Kitchen Table

A kitchen table often becomes a short-term desk—sometimes for business and sometimes for household accounts. If a chandelier is mandated over the kitchen table that could double as a desk, choose a chandelier with a downlight. A chandelier is normally hung over

Screen and copy...

...equal in value.

the center of a table and is not intended for extended use. This position can create reflected glare on reading/writing tasks. Likewise, a downlight pendant can create a glare. If reading materials are usually glossy, use portable fixtures for the duration of the task.

Computers are used at kitchen tables. All the principles of lighting computers apply to kitchen tables. Temporary portable fixtures can be brought to the kitchen table to illuminate the hardcopy input, if enough glare-free light is available to light the surroundings.

At kitchen tabletops used as a desk, both nearby and farther away illumination give the needed balance. Create high-quality desk lighting at home. Whether it is a dedicated desk or a tabletop used as a short-term desk, it is an office.

For Television

Television screens are getting bigger and are used in many spaces. Big or small, they are frequently located in kitchens. If so, the screen acts like a mirror, reflecting any direct light

Never light a wine rack.

source (chandelier) or brightly lighted surface (uplight on ceiling) in view. Hence, assure that the TV can be seen without glare from the typical places in the kitchen, both seated and standing. Design the lighting so that it will not reflect on the screen. Not-so-visible fixtures are the best. If ceilings or walls are lighted, specify more general illumination to avoid brightness from these surfaces. If all else fails, specify a TV with a nonreflecting screen.

For Wet Bars

Lighting for wet bars in kitchens (or other rooms) can be the same as lighting for kitchen sinks and inside cabinets. The objects in the bar—glass and polished metal—sparkle in direct light. Often shelving is glass and can transmit the light. Frequently, glass shelves are backed up with mirrored walls. Be careful of glare from direct lights reflecting from mirrors to other locations, seated or standing, in the room.

In bars, incandescent downlights are suitable sources, because unlike furniture cabinets, heat buildup is usually not a problem and the punch of incandescent light is needed to penetrate multiple glass shelves. Decorative low-voltage tubes or strips are also good. Above the countertop, the back or the sides of the bar can be a luminous panel with decorative architectural glass or plastic. Fluorescent, cold cathode, fiber optics, or MR source and prismatic material can light the panel. In addition, linear fluorescent can be above the header at the wet bar recess, giving hidden general illumination.

Likewise, stemware racks can have low-voltage strips to emphasize their existence. Racks inside cabinets should have ¼-watt sources to minimize heat buildup. Racks below cabinets can have more watts depending upon the need to attract attention with bright light at the rack. Brightness attracts attention.

Never, never light wine storage racks or put lighting inside unrefrigerated wine cabinets. The quality of wine is highly dependant upon low temperature storage. Good wine needs to be protected while it matures. All lighting gives off heat; do not use it. Ready-made wine coolers have interior lighting, but they refrigerate to keep wine at the proper temperature.

End-lit fiber optics can decoratively accent countertops, backsplashes, or other surfaces in bars. (See *Decorative-Effect Fixtures* in Chapter 5.) Wet bars are classy and should be shown in the best light.

nontask surfaces

Light for the Room Itself

Sometimes the room can be illuminated sufficiently by light from the sink, stove, and other work locations, but sometimes not. Cooks will want to see easily into upper and lower cabinets and may require more sources. Several alternatives are available.

If the upper cabinets do not go all the way to the ceiling, cove lighting can be installed on the top of the built-in upper cabinets in fitted kitchens or tall case pieces in unfitted kitchens with excellent results. Cove lighting consists of fluorescent channels that bounce light off the ceiling and spread it around the room. Collectibles or usable kitchen objects can be displayed above the cabinets and lighted either from the front (highlighting color and shape) or from behind (silhouetted). Choose whichever lighting looks best and installs easiest. (See *Coves* in Chapter 5.)

If cabinets do not go all the way to the ceiling, custom make a dropped soffit above and in front of upper cabinets. Soffits have increased in popularity threefold, according to a National Kitchen and Bath Association study, and rightfully so. They delivers excellent upper-cabinet lighting. (See *Dropped Soffits* in Chapter 5.) Or purchase ready-made wall brackets as a soffit for the same position.

A center-ceiling fixture can be either surface mounted or recessed. A recessed fixture is less obvious, particulary if the diffuser lens or louver is not overly bright. A recessed fixture with a dropped lens spreads some light on the ceiling; a flat lens sends light down. A parabolic louver is the least bright. Some surface-mounted fixtures permit light to come through the sides of the fixture; some do not. If the fixture can be seen from another room, choose one that does not send light through the sides. When used alone, too much glare

Cabinets support cove lighting.

Center-ceiling light illuminates the center of the room.

would be created, because the light would contrast with the darkness. The larger the center-ceiling fixture is, the less bright it is and the more comfortable to view. A center-ceiling fixture illuminates the center of the room, which in most kitchens is empty. Therefore, light should not be overly bright and attract attention. Work locations should be brighter. Countertops always look better than floors. If the center is not empty and contains an island or a peninsula, install the ceiling fixture directly above. (See *Ready-Made Recessed Fixtures* in Chapter 5.)

In small windowless kitchens, luminous ceilings are excellent. They provide broadly spread room lighting from low-energy-consuming fluorescent channels. They must be augmented by countertop lighting; otherwise, the cook creates his or her own shadow. (See *Luminous Panels* in Chapter 5.)

If one or more walls have large windows, an up- and downlight valance over the draperies or other window treatment can spread light. Do not use over bare windows. No light will be reflected. (See *Valances* in Chapter 5.)

Luminous ceilings for small kitchens.

If a wall is highly textured, graze it with light. Likewise, if the cabinet doors are textured (raised or recessed panel, board and batten, or tambour), graze them with light. Light shows off their well-done details. Use open incandescent downlights, keeping the wattage low to avoid heat. Also, as much as possible, make sure that the scallop of light falls on each cabinet in the same place. Nothing destroys the aesthetics of lighting as quickly as poorly positioned scallops from downlights. (See *Wall Grazing* in Chapter 1 and *Underline Wall Texture with Grazing* in Chapter 5.)

See for Yourself #10: Where Will the Scallop Fall?

1. Draw an elevation of the upper cabinets to scale.
2. Draw the recessed downlights in the estimated positions.
3. Determine the beam spread of the lamps from the manufacturer's catalog. Draw the spreads on the elevation.
4. Check to assure that the scallops of light will not disadvantage the aesthetics.

If a wall is covered with a special wallpaper or fabric, wall wash it. (See *Wall Washing* in Chapter 1 and see *Cornices* and *Recessed Perimeter Coffer* in Chapter 5.) Cornice lighting is particularly good in kitchens emulating a period style. In perimeter troughs and cornices, use low-wattage line-voltage or fluorescent sources.

Luminous Panels

A luminous panel can be used between the countertop and upper cabinet as a backsplash or between two upper cabinets as a cornice. Both provide not only light but also a decorative ambience. The panel can be glass or plastic. For the backsplash position, choose panel colors that do not impart a distinct hue to the light. Red, green, or blue, for example, would make food look odd. For the cornice position, choose any hue. The light below will still be white, and the light transmitted through the panel will be colorful without causing interference. In the backsplash position, a panel can be illuminated by fluorescent channels or with prismatic film and a single MR source. Build a box. If fluorescent, place them at the top and bottom, or at the left and right sides.

A leaded-glass luminous panel.

Leaded.

Beveled.

Etched.

Abraxis Art Glass

If the panel material is transparent, place the lamps 4 inches back from the edges so that they will not show. To obtain even light, the box should be one-sixth as deep as the distance between the channels. For example, if the channels are 21 inches apart, the box depth could be 3½ inches. Hinge the panel so that the lamps can be replaced when they burn out, usually not sooner than three years.

If MR, position back from the edges, where accessible to change the lamp. The base cabinet would be suitable. Paint the inside of the box flat white. Moreover, plan how you want to control the luminous panel; a wall switch is the most convenient. (See *Luminous Panels* in Chapter 5.)

Inside Cabinet Lighting

Fitted-kitchen upper cabinets sometimes have leaded, beveled, etched, or clear glass doors. In unfitted kitchens, tall furniture (breakfronts, pie safes, etc.) often have glass or pierced panel doors. At night, such cabinets appear black. Why not put lighting inside? Several distributions are possible: accent, backlight, frontlight, and uplight. For accenting, use low-wattage (25 or less) MR or R sources. Avoid single, higher-wattage light sources recessed into the top of the furniture or cabinets, even with glass shelves. Heat builds up. Unless crackers and cereal are stored inside, heat is unwelcome.

Renters (or owners) can use miniature, shelf-edge, track fixtures with 7-watt, line-voltage lamps in upper cabinets. They are hung on each shelf and are removable.

For back-, front-, and uplighting, use either fluorescent lamps (subminiature or mini-bipin) or low-voltage lamps in tubes.

Backlighting.

Accent lighting.

Frontlighting.

Low voltage has small wires and the tubes could be glued in place, thereby doing the least damage to antique furniture. Hide all fixtures well back from the sides of the door, out of view. Switch them together at a central location for a soft effect, even when the room is not occupied.

Whatever the position, hide the fixture behind a structural portion of the cabinet or a piece of added wood trim.

Tambour cabinets often hold large appliances at countertop levels. These cabinets are called appliance garages. They are deep and might need inside-cabinet lighting. A mini-bipin fluorescent or low-voltage tube at the front of the cabinet would light the inside.

Light Distribution Inside Cabinets

- To backlight, tuck lamps neatly behind furred-out shelves or below the shelves.
- To accent, place lamps on the left or right inside cabinet doors.
- To uplight, secure at the front of the shelf to hurl light up.
- To frontlight, put lamps at the front of the shelf above.

Lighted cabinets yield soft light.

Expand the kitchen with outside lighting.

St. Charles

Light Outside the Room

In one- or two-floor residences with more than zero lot lines if the kitchen has large windows, light the outside. First, light outside balances the interior light to prevent the windows from turning into black mirrors at night. The amount of light inside and out should be equal. However, any bright surface (the ceiling) or any visible sources (a bare-lamp chandelier) will reflect on the window regardless of how carefully the balance is planned. Reduce the interior brightness to and increase outside brightness prevent glare.

Second, light outside expands the vista of the kitchen. Use accent lighting on pleasing exterior objects, architectural or landscape materials. If trees are tall and have many leaves, downlight through the leaves onto the ground creates patterns of light and shadows—called moonlighting. It has great appeal. Many landscape lighting companies have maintenance contracts to replace lamps so owners do not have to climb trees. Do not miss out on expanding the kitchen space with outside lighting.

Appliance garages may need light.

Wilsonart

Accenting

Decorative items in kitchens deserve accent light. Incandescent sources accent the best, but they also fade colors. Precious art should not be exposed to incandescent light without an ultraviolet filter. Fluorescent light fades colors less. However, highlights and shadows are lost. Take your choice. If fading is not a serious problem recessed, adjustable incandescent downlights, particularly low voltage, are good. A track fixture can be canopy mounted on the surface and do the same thing. For renters, portable adjustable luminaires are suitable.

Accent special tile murals in backsplashes. Heighten tile colors and bring the mural to life at night. If the tile is glossy, accent at a steep angle to avoid glare.

Often, kitchens have fireplaces. Some are elaborate with pizza ovens and barbecues; others are covered with decorative tiles. Accent any special fireplace. Do not let it fade away with the walls at night. Accent light creates a focal point giving warmth even when the fireplace is not used.

Accent artwork.

Wilsonart

Ceiling downlights accent brass rails.

Low-wattage, bay-window light as a nightlight.

In kitchens with metal railings at countertop edges, accent light creates highlights and sparkle on the metal, justifying the expense and intensifying the decorative effect. Traditional kitchens have brass rails; contemporary kitchens have chrome.

In kitchen eating areas, accent only the table surface with bright light and have darkness beyond, creating an intimate atmosphere and drawing people to the table. Use incandescent downlight, line or low voltage. (See *Carve Out a Space Within a Space* in Chapter 5.)

If plant materials are included in the decor, low-voltage strings are excellent. In addition, portable adjustable uplights can illuminate the foliage and create a shadow pattern on a plain wall for an additional accent.

With bay or boxed windows, consider accenting the window with soft light, turned on at night even when the space is not occupied. Do it with 25-watt, line- or low-voltage incandescent. It creates a warm ambience from the outside and inside. (See *Punctuate a Distinctive Small Area with Satiny Light* in Chapter 5.)

Countertops, backsplashes, walls, and ceilings can be accented with end-lit fiber optics. The ends of the fibers are flush with the surface and create beads of light. The source is a single MR source, which can have a color filter or a color wheel. (See *Decorative-Effect Fixtures* in Chapter 5.)

Likewise, low-voltage tubes, panels, and strings can create accents. The tubes can outline unusual architectural features such as stemware racks hanging below cabinets, a skylight on the ceiling, or latticework. Panels can be installed on the ceiling or wall, creating starlike glitter. Strings can be threaded through interior plants. (See *Decorative-Effect Fixtures* in Chapter 5.)

Accent special fireplaces.

dimmers and energy

Programmable Dimmers

All fixtures in a kitchen do not need to be used at the same time. However, I had one client who insisted that the kitchen lights be all on or all off. She did not want to switch lights at different locations no matter how convenient. Contrary to this feeling, the advantage of multiple lighting is that lights can be used alone or in combination, creating different scenes. Multiple lighting is energy efficient; unused light can be turned off. Multiple lighting can be controlled with switches at the fixtures, with wall switches, or with a programmable dimmer.

A programmable dimmer can control multiple fixtures with up to 2,000 watts from one or more locations. The master location has dimmers that combine the light levels of the various fixtures. The program stores the combinations. Both the master and the remote locations have switches that connect one or more dimmers together to create different scenes. One scene for a kitchen could be low, soft light to permit finding the ice and hors d'oeuvres. Another scene could be all sources on brightly for serious pot scrubbing. A third scene could be bright light focused on the eating surface and soft light at countertops where cooking clutter goes unnoticed. These scenes can be turned on or off by additional wall switches and by a remote control. Typically, programmable dimmers have either 3 or 4 dimmers and scene switches. Further, they have a fade rate, usually 5 seconds, but some can fade on or off for 15 seconds. A nice touch! Programmable dimmers work well for open kitchens or for kitchens that host frequent parties with easily obtainable, preprogrammed, and impressive lighting ambiences.

Low, soft light to find
ice and hors d'oeuvres.

Siematic

High, bright light
to scrub pots and pans.

Siematic

Energy Conservation

Some states are determined to reduce energy consumption. California, for instance, requires that the ambient or general lighting in kitchens (and baths) be energy efficient—the source must produce at least 40 lumens per watt. Fluorescent meets this requirement. Incandescent does not. But only linear are allowable. Screw-based compact fluorescent are not permitted, because they can be easily interchanged for energy-inefficient incandescent after the electrical inspection. In addition, fluorescent must be connected to the first accessible wall switch. Other sources (fluorescent or incandescent) for localized lighting can be connected to the second or third switches. Other state (or national) codes are based on maximum allowable watts per square foot of space, particularly in high-rise residences. They usually apply to laundry rooms, too. Some states regulate minimum efficiencies acceptable for fixtures. These methods get at the same problem—wasted energy.

The local building inspector's office can supply information on energy and special fixture requirements for closets, damp locations, and other potentially hazardous locations.

All in all, the whole kitchen can be pleasingly lighted with fluorescent. Choose warm-white deluxe or 30° or 35°K prime-color sources. They render colors well and blend with incandescent in other spaces. Prime color costs about three times more but is worth considering. Kitchen surfaces are used 365 days each year and the additional cost would be less than a half a cent a day for the life of the lamp. Sell the long-term benefits. Kitchen lighting lasts a long time.

chapter

8

lighting baths with electric light

Bathrooms that are less than 65 square feet are considered small. Bathrooms that are more than 65 square feet are considered large. Whatever the square footage, the average bathroom costs six thousand dollars. The cost can go as high as thirty thousand with deluxe products, according to the *Kitchen and Bath Business* magazine. For small or large baths, a tub costs between two hundred and five-thousand dollars. Surely no one would object to spending two to five hundred dollars on lighting the bath.

Bathrooms are hard to light. Bathroom fixtures seem limited, but many lighting choices are available. The effect of good lighting on the quality and ease of grooming and ambience of the space are worth the effort to design bathroom lighting well.

Typical bathrooms have built-in base cabinets with countertops and porcelain or fiberglass plumbing products. However, manufacturers are producing furniture to be used as base cabinets for drop-in lavatories, permitting traditional styles to be carried into bathrooms. Never before has so much pe-riod-style furniture for bathrooms been manufactured. They are available in Country English, Victorian, Edwardian, Queen Anne, and Shaker styles. The manufacturers are giving an opportunity for contemporary convenience with finely-detailed, antique reproductions. In addition, many bath designers are using authentic antiques—sideboards, credenzas, low boys, and console tables—to hold lavatories with elaborate crystal, porcelain, or gold faucets for traditional bathrooms.

Whether contemporary or traditional, bathrooms contain mirrors, tubs, showers, closets, and sometimes exercise areas. All require light. Light for mirrors must be on the person—the task surface—not on the mirror. Light for tasks in tubs, showers, and clothes must be in the tubs, showers, or closets. Light for exercise areas should be reflected, not direct, to avoid glare.

In addition, decorative items could be enhanced with accent light and textured wall surfaces with grazing light. General illumination for the bath could come from the total of task and nontask light. Otherwise, general

Typical bathroom.

Traditional bathroom.

room illumination is needed. Some states have energy requirements for baths, restricting the use of inefficient light sources or fixtures. Moreover, the National Electric Code requires a ground fault interrupter on the circuit for a wall receptacle within 6 feet of water in water.

It protects people from getting a shock from their electric appliances. (Install them for your own bath, too.) Finally, many states and local codes require waterproof fixtures. Comply with all these safety requirements. Be safe rather than sorry.

task surfaces

Faces in Mirrors

The task surface at mirrors is the face reflected in the mirror, not the surface of the mirror. Often people want to light the mirror itself, but light must fall on the face (and hair), the surfaces needed to be seen in the mirror.

Individual differences, such as preferences, age, eye conditions, and interior colors, play a big part in choosing the type and amount of lighting for mirrors. Some people prefer wall-hung fixtures beside the mirror. Most have preferences about the color of light. Incandescent light (red) enhances perceived facial colors in our culture, whatever the skin color. In Eastern cultures, red is not consid-

ered flattering; white (from blue light) enhancement is.

Fluorescent can enhance reds also, if warm-white deluxe or 30° or 35°K prime-color lamps are used. Such lamps produce more red, than do cool white. However, people who work in offices lighted by cool white may want cool white to apply makeup. They are seen under such light all day long. (See *Color of Fluorescent Light* in Chapter 4.) Some portable makeup mirrors are made to light both ways.

Older users require more light, between twice and two-thirds more. Some users are nearsighted and an illuminated magnifying mirror helps.

Interior colors affect the color of light.

At mirrors, the tint of the interior color can have a profound effect. To this point, one South Florida resident wrote to my newspaper column inquiring as to why her skin tone appeared different in two bathrooms equipped with the same kind of bare lamps at the mirrors. In one bath, her skin tone looked true; in the other, her skin appeared sallow. The reason was the color of the walls, a sunshine yellow, reflecting an unflattering hue on her. In bathrooms, do not cover a wall adjacent to the mirror with a color that does not flatter. Light, whatever the source, will pick up a tint of that color and reflect it on the face.

MIRRORS ABOVE LAVATORIES

A lavatory can be freestanding as a pedestal, dropped into a built-in countertop or antique furniture, or wall-hung for decorative or for wheelchair reasons.

The bathroom mirror is usually on the wall above the lavatory. The size of the mirror determines which lighting fixtures should be used, and the status of ownership determines how the fixtures can be installed. Owners can more easily install hard-wired fixtures connected to the electricity in the wall or ceiling. Renters, on the other hand, must use plug-in fixtures. Either way, the fixtures should control the brightness, light the top of the head, and distribute the light along the side of the face and under the chin, particularly for visual shavers. (However, some men shave without looking.)

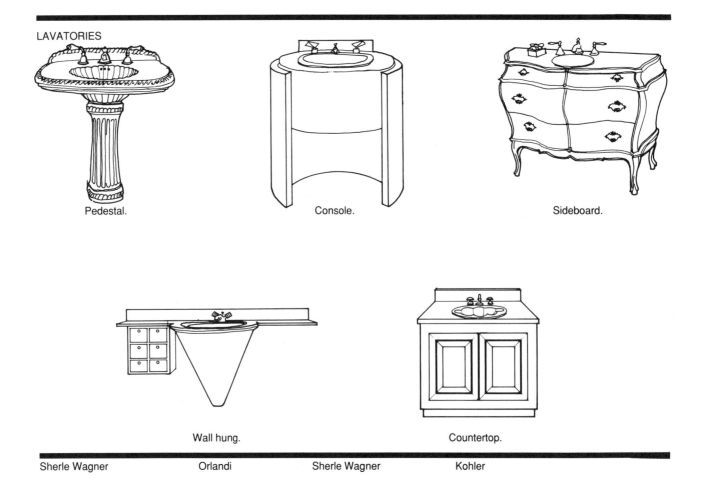

LAVATORIES

Pedestal.

Console.

Sideboard.

Wall hung.

Countertop.

Sherle Wagner   Orlandi   Sherle Wagner   Kohler

Small Mirrors

Lighting small mirrors is difficult because fixtures beside the mirror are in view. Any bright source of light within view causes glare and inhibits seeing the less-bright details in the mirror. On the one hand, if the bathroom is period style with an antique (Bombé chest, French-burled walnut server, or English side table) or a reproduction (Queen Anne wooden vanity, Hepplewhite side table, or Edwardian marble console) with a lavatory, the solutions are deeply recessed downlights with wide-beam lamps, a cove or valance reflecting uplight softly, wall-mounted fixtures, or table-top portable fixtures. (See the various fixtures in Chapter 5 and *Mirrors at Dressing Tables or Dressers* in this chapter.) Today more than ever before, historic style can be easily brought into the bath.

On the other hand, if the bathroom is not historic style, the best solution is to broadly spread light with fluorescent sources reflecting from as many surfaces around the mirror as possible, particularly the custom-made ways.

Dropped Canopy

A dropped canopy hung from the ceiling with two or four fluorescent lamps distributes light below and above. Hang it 10 inches down from the ceiling. Use a lens below and leave open above. Light will bounce off the ceiling, the walls, and countertop (if available). Fluorescent sources need not be cool white. A wide range of color choices are available that enhance facial colors and distinguish beard from skin. (See *Color of Fluorescent* in Chapter 4 and *Canopy* in Chapter 5.)

Behind the Mirror

Use linear sources, either fluorescent or incandescent and choose a length that is at least two-thirds as long as the mirror's dimension (width or height). Mount the mirror on a wooden frame, furring it out 4 inches from the wall. Make the frame 4 inches smaller than the dimensions of the mirror and 4 inches deep. Attach the lamps to the frame, at the top, the bottom, and the two sides. Stand the mirror off the wall with brackets.

A canopy reflects light from many surfaces.

Dramatic and flattering light behind a mirror.

Chapter Eight **113**

Use this lighting when the mirror is between two sidewalls or the view of the mirror profile is blocked by partitions; otherwise, the 4-inch furred out space will be visible and will not be as effective as it could be if hidden. The mirror will be surrounded by a halo of light and appear to float. The soft light will be particularly flattering to faces, creating a desirable illusion.

Furred-out mirror
section and elevation.

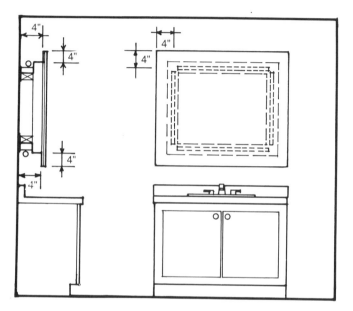

Luminous panels above
and at the sides.

From the Sides and Above
Mirrors are sometimes built into a closet or into a small recess at the countertop with sidewalls and a dropped ceiling. If so, light the mirror from the sides and above with luminous panels. (See *Arch Reveals or Recess Lighting* in Chapter 5.) Use either an opal diffuser with fluorescent or cold cathode, or use a single MR source and prismatic material. Both spread soft light in the recess area, lighting the sides and above the face, the best possible mirror lighting.

READY-MADE WAYS TO DO IT

On the Wall at Each Side and Above the Mirror
On the wall at each side and above the mirror, use incandescent or fluorescent with opal-glass lenses, translucent shades, or well-diffused bare lamps (coated, low wattage, and placed well out of direct view). Fluorescent is preferable because it provides good distribu-

tion for little energy—20 watts on each side and 80 watts above for a total of 120 watts and 15 percent extra for the ballast.

Incandescent would require three times as many watts to do the same job. Also, incandescent produces heat. If incandescent-style fixtures are required for the decor, lamp them with compact fluorescent lamps if the shade is translucent or opaque. If opaque shades are used, be sure to include additional light in the space to prevent glare. If transparent shades are used, use only clear, decorative incandescent lamps. Clear-glass covers demand low-wattage, clear-glass lamps. (See *Lamps for Decorative Fixtures* in Chapter 4.)

Above the Mirror (and/or at the Sides)
Fixtures with lenses can be used above and/or at the sides of the mirror. To comply with the California Energy Code, one California fixture manufacturer has made 1 to 4 fluorescent-lamped fixtures, using only 10 watts each. The lens softens the light and obscures seeing the open-bent compact tube. These fixtures have an electronic ballast, also. They give an energy-saving, good light option to people in

all states.

Fixtures with bare lamps can be used above and/or at the sides of the mirror, if they are low wattage. Use additional light sources in the space to dilute the brightness. Line-voltage G lamps in 5 to 15 watts are good. Silvered-bowl G lamps in higher wattage reflect the light from the wall. Low-voltage G lamps in 2½ to 5 watts might be better. But low-voltage lamps must be hooked up to an accessible transformer. Mount it in a cabinet, a closet behind the wall, or the attic above. Both line and low voltage in low wattage can be glare free. Low-wattage lamps mean less glare. High-wattage lamps mean more glare.

If nonclear lamps are used, coated, not frosted, lamps produce the least glare. Also, a fixture as long as the mirror with an opal lens and higher wattage lamps can give good light to the face without glare. Likewise, a ready-made bracket fixture sending light up to the ceiling and down can light a mirror without glare.

Bare lights
beside a mirror.

Opal-glass lenses are best.

Hanging at the Sides

Translucent pendants at eye level can be hung at the sides of small mirrors, if aesthetically pleasing. Low-wattage lamps and opal shades are recommended. If transparent shades are chosen, use clear lamps, not over 15 watts, and preferably 7, with additional light sources in the space. If translucent shades are chosen, wattage can be higher. However, be sure the color of the light imparted through the shade is flattering. Erté, a French artist famous for art deco figures of women, sold many bronze-glass hand mirrors for flattering reflections to high-end clients.

Medicine-Cabinet Mirrors

Several manufacturers have designed attractive lighted medicine cabinets. The best have well-shielded light sources. They can supply reasonable light for the mirror, but are obvious. Inspect them lighted before ordering.

Ready-made pendants.

Custom-made pendants.

For a design challenge, use only portable fixtures.

Portable Fixtures

In historic structures or new structures with period-style interiors, portable fixtures can light the mirror area if chosen with care about distribution and quality of light. (See *Mirrors at Dressing Tables or Dressers* in this chapter.) For a design challenge, light the whole period-style bathroom with portable fixtures. It can be done, but not without skillful planning.

Large Mirrors

If a mirror is 3 feet or more wide above a countertop, it helps reflect the light. Large mirrors look appropriate with large fixtures. Linear fluorescent fixtures are large. They can be custom made or ready-made. Owners may want to build a soffit or bracket to hold fluorescent lamps. A soffit directs light down, reflecting it from the countertop and sidewalls to the face. Likewise, the bracket directs it down and also up, if desired to illuminate the ceiling. A ready-made surface-mounted ceiling fixture can be used by owners who choose not to custom build lighting or by renters who cannot custom build. A ceiling fixture over the mirror provides light in the same way as a soffit or bracket. Renters can connect them to a track hooked up to the electricity through a ceiling junction box where a ceiling fixture is now located.

CUSTOM-MADE WAYS TO DO IT

Dropped Soffit

A dropped soffit is a boxed-in area of a ceiling dropped 8 to 12 inches down, preferably between two sidewalls. Dropped soffits look best above a countertop and should be the same length (left to right), but not the same depth (front to back) as the top. The soffit can be 12 to 18 inches deep and should be able to hold a diffuser to scatter the light or a louver to block the view of the lamps. For small bathrooms, use a louver, because it is unaffected by the change of air pressure with the door opening and closing. Use two singles or a double fluorescent channel, unless the room has medium- to dark-colored walls or unless the eyes require more light. If so, use reflectors behind the lamps or three or four

fluorescent lamps. Paint the inside of the soffit flat white to reflect light. The exterior surface should be finished to blend with the bathroom walls, and the bottom should blend with the ceiling. For example, a soffit could be built of sheetrock, plastered, painted off-white on the bottom to match the ceiling, and wallpapered on the outside to match the walls. (See *Dropped Soffits* in Chapter 5.)

Bracket

A bracket is a cantilevered shelf holding lights. Like a dropped soffit, it looks best above a countertop. It should be the same length as the top, be at least 10 inches down from the ceiling to allow adequate reflection, and be 14 to 18 inches deep. The faceboard should be at least 6 inches high and covered with any material that enhances the interior decor—wood, tiles, wallpaper, fabric, or paint. Use two single fluorescent channels, one on the inside of the faceboard at the top and one on the wall. The distance from the end of the channel to the end of the bracket, ideally, should be no more than 6 inches in order to

A dropped soffit puts light down.

Brackets for high ceilings.

have smooth lighting. Paint the inside of the faceboard flat white. Use a diffuser at the bottom. For less light on the ceiling, use white perforated metal on the top, covering just the fluorescent lamp at the wall or covering both lamps, depending on how much light is desirable on the ceiling. (See *Brackets* Chapter 5.)

Fixtures for Small Mirrors
Fixtures described for small mirrors (wall sconces, bare-lamp holders, etc.) are also suitable for large mirrors when the proportions are right and suitably lamped. Mount small fixtures directly on the mirror. Or mount vertical linear fixtures as dividers to segment the mirror. Lamp them will low-wattage to avoid glare.

Ceiling-Mounted Decorative Fixtures
Three-way mirrors from the countertop to the ceiling look great with several, small ceiling-mounted decorative fixtures. The optimum number of fixtures depends upon the ceiling space and the proportions of the fixtures. Do not overpower the vanity area; make the scene subtle. The fixtures reflect and rereflect in all the mirrors, appearing to be infinite in number. Be sure to lamp the fixtures with low-wattage to avoid glare from so many reflections. Also, plan for additional fixtures to light the rest of the bathroom.

Small Chandeliers
A small guest bathroom is enhanced with a small chandelier hung off center in front of a large mirror, reflecting soft glitter. In bathrooms used daily, the chandelier must be augmented by additional mirror lighting. The chandelier can be separately switched for use when guests are expected.

Angled walls with three ceiling-mounted fixtures.

Mount wall fixtures on the mirror.

Nulco

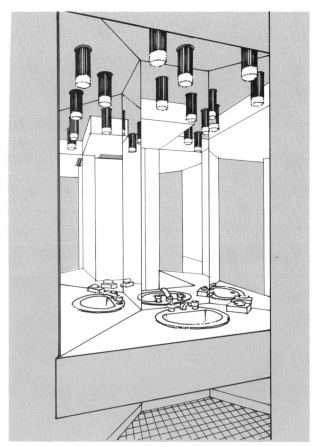

H.H. Angus

A small chandelier in front of a large mirror enhances a small bathroom.

Segment a large mirror with linear sources. Alkco

Linear Sources

Large mirrors can be vertically segmented with linear sources (either fluorescent with a lens or dimmed linear incandescent) for good mirror lighting. Linear incandescent are made to recess between the segments with silver, black, or gold lamp holders and matching backings without lamps to reach from the bottom to the top of the mirror. Like fluorescent, linear incandescent wattage is tied to the length. The longest is 41 inches at 150 watts—too bright for most situations. Consequently, provide a dimmer or better yet, fix the dimmed amount with a preset slide dimmer so that the owner cannot adjust beyond a pleasing brightness.

MIRRORS ELSEWHERE

Mirrors at Dressing Tables or Dressers

Mirrors at a dressing table or dresser are commonly lighted by portable fixtures. The design of the fixture and shade is not just a matter of aesthetics but of function. If the shade is opaque, narrow at the top, and broad at the bottom, it squeezes the light down, illuminating the top of the dresser, not the face. Choose a shade that transmits light and is 2 inches taller than the lamp (bulb). If the portable fixture is tall enough, it will illuminate the face well; if it is too short, glare gets into the eyes. It almost cannot be too tall, unless the bottom of the shade is above eye level.

Translucent shade.

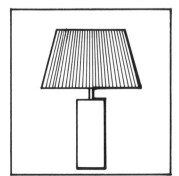

Shade wide at top and bottom.

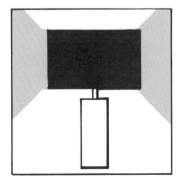

Shade narrow at top and wide at bottom.

Experiment with various wattages to get the exact amount of light desired. Instead of incandescent, consider using a fluorescent adapter and a bipin-based or screw-based compact fluorescent. Both emit more than three times as much light as incandescent and consume at the least one-third less electricity.

Full-Length Mirror or Mirrored Closet Doors

A full-length mirror can be hung on a wall or closet doors, or be freestanding. Ideally, the fixture that lights a full-length mirror should be out of sight, but should illuminate the person from head to toe—hard to do. Downlights on the ceiling above the head cast unpleasant shadows on the face. Surface-mounted ceiling fixtures can cause glare if not balanced by additional general illumination. Wall fixtures need wall space, which usually is not available. Also, wall fixtures close to a mirror can cause glare by being directly in the line of sight. Uplight on the ceiling is better. It casts well-spread light on the whole person at the mirror.

Uplight for mirrors is best.

A downlight in 8-foot ceilings should be close to the mirror and have a diffuser to soften shadows under the eyebrows, nose, and chin. Recessed fixtures are architecturally out of the way and aesthetically do not attract unnecessary attention to themselves.

A diffusing surface-mounted ceiling fixture could provide good light, if it is not the only light in the space.

If on the wall, one fixture could be above the mirror or two fixtures on the sides. Some may desire bare lamps; use low wattage and consider low voltage. Generally, opal lenses are the best. Translucent wall fixtures should

diffuse the light and not be mounted on a dark wall.

Uplight, the best lighting method, could come from wall sconces, wall brackets, coves, or pendants. Mount wall sconces on either side of the mirror above standing eye level. A wall bracket could be above the mirror. To throw light the farthest, a wall-mounted cove needs to have an angled faceboard or an angled block below the fluorescent channel. A cove in the top of a freestanding closet does not need an angled faceboard to throw the light. An uplight pendant could hang at the top of the mirror and illuminate the ceiling. If at all possible, use uplight at full-length mirrors.

Mirrored Walls

Some bathrooms have one or more walls mirrored, especially if exercise takes place there. If so, use glare-free lighting. Any decorative fixture would reflect glare in the mirror. Cove lighting, ready-made or custom-made, is glare free. It is indirect. It is composed of a cove board on one or two walls, with linear lamps behind it. Install the cove board at least 10 inches down from the ceiling to bounce as much light off the ceiling as possible. The ceiling then becomes a large light source softly

Wilsonart

Sunrise Specialty

reflecting in the mirror, not glaring. (See *Coves* in Chapter 5.)

Likewise, recessed or surface-mounted perimeter fluorescent lighting will light a mirrored bathroom or exercise area glare free. (See *Recessed Perimeter Coffer* in Chapter 5.)

Since many exercises are done lying on one's back, facing the ceiling, do not position any ceiling-recessed or surface-mounted fixtures directly over an exercise bench or mat location.

Bodies in Tubs, Whirlpools, and Showers

Bodies in tubs, whirlpools, or showers require light. Most often tubs and showers do not have a light source. The fixture must be watertight and should be recessed in the ceiling. The light helps with washing, grooming, and reading instructions on labels. Many of my clients who initially are somewhat unconvinced, cheer resoundingly after installing a tub or shower light, and wonder how they got along without one before.

A California company has incorporated an open-bent compact lamp into a covered recessed fixture with a diffuser. It is 21 watts and equals the light from a 100-watt incandescent. It meets the energy-efficiency codes in California and should be used in other states also. (Avoid legislation and design energy efficiently now.)

Sometimes a tub is an elaborate bathroom feature and deserves special lighting effects. If the bathroom is not a period style, low-voltage tube lights are good at creating an effect and can be made waterproof. An owner who has a bathroom with the ceiling directly below the roof can build in a skylight to illuminate the tub during the daytime and have low-voltage tube lights around the skylight to illuminate it at night. In contrast, an authentic period-style bathroom (like one with a Victorian claw-and-ball-foot tub and an oval, brass shower-curtain rod) needs a watertight, ceiling-mounted decorative fixture or light reflecting from the ceiling from a cove fixture. In another style, a domed cove with a pen-

A domed cove with uplight.

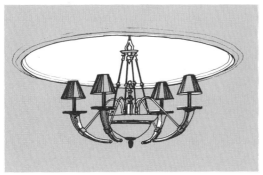

Focal Point and Nulco

Luminous Ceiling Installation

1. Panel should be minimally 6 inches deep. The deeper the box, the more uniform the brightness of the light on the diffusing material.
2. Whatever the depth, position the fluorescent lamps apart by a distance equal to one and a half times the depth of the box. Allow half that distance to the edge of the box. Therefore, if the box is 6 inches deep, the fluorescent fixtures should be 9 inches apart and 4½ inches from the edge of the box on each side.
3. The grid (custom-built or ready-made commercial grid systems) with the diffusing material (opal plastic lens or translucent leaded glass) should be made as watertight as possible. The grid should accommodate the size of the diffusing material.

dant uplight could reflect light from the ceiling over a tub without a shower.

In contemporary style baths, a luminous ceiling or recessed fluorescent skylight can create a skylight effect and provide a large surface of light. For a luminous ceiling, use linear fluorescent and space them evenly behind a translucent diffusing panel. The diffuser can be held in place by a wood or metal grid. The panel should be the same size as the ceiling over the tub or shower. (See *Fluorescent Skylights and Troffers* and *Luminous Panels* in Chapter 5.)

Some local codes might reject this custom-made fixture as not being waterproof enough. If so, a few well-designed, ready-made luminous ceilings or recessed fluorescent skylights are available.

If the tub or shower area is embellished with plants, a luminous ceiling can keep the plants healthy, when turned on for 14 hours a day and equipped with cool-white lamps. The area will be very appealing both day and night, and the temptation will be to take more leisurely baths or showers.

Luminous ceiling.

Sample Electric Cost

A 40-watt fluorescent light, including ballast, can be on for 14 hours per day for $1.93 per month, if electricity costs 10¢ per kilowatt-hour.

Never use an open downlight above a tub or shower. Cold water and hot glass do not mix, the glass shatters.

Reading at the Toilet

Some people read in the bathroom. If they read at the toilet and it is in a recess with two sidewalls, mount a custom- or ready-made bracket fixture on the back wall for both up- and downlight. Use a linear fluorescent lamp or two, depending upon the wall colors and/ or the age of the user. Likewise, a custom- or ready-made cove fixture could give good uplight for reading. Moreover, two wall sconces, on the left and right, could provide light.

If the toilet is not in a recess, a downlight mounted over the front edge is suitable.

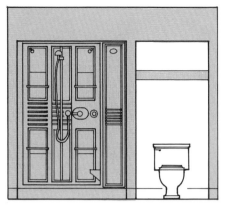
A bracket fixture for a toilet recess.

Jacuzzi

In Clothes Closets

Light is mandatory in clothes closets for inspecting, selecting, and finding. Consequently, all closets 10 or more square feet should have a light.

Closet Lights

- a recessed fixture with a lens
- a porcelain socket mounted on the inside above the door header with an A lamp
- a surface-mounted fluorescent fixture on the ceiling two-thirds the width of the closet

---

With louvered closet doors, use bare-lamp fluorescent, enhanced with an asymmetric reflector. Such a system backlights the slats in louvered doors. Control the fluorescent fixtures with a wall switch or an automatic switch activated by the door opening or closing. Control a porcelain socket and a bare A lamp mounted on the door header with a pull chain directly on the fixture. Keep the A lamp 12 inches away from anything combustible. (Some codes will not permit a bare lamp in a closet.)

Sometimes closets have built-in dressers and mirrors. If so, bare G lamps on channels can illuminate them. Equip the channels with 5-watt lamps or less, so that the closet area will not be glaring or hot from high-wattage lamps. In addition, the closet sidewalls can have recessed, custom-made luminous panels. Use either fluorescent or cold cathode with an opal diffuser, or a single MR source and prismatic material. Both are cool. Both spread soft light beautifully from the sides. (See *Arch Reveals or Recess Lighting* in Chapter 5.)

For Television

Television sets are often in bathrooms. (They certainly are in the better hotels.) However, the sets are usually small with small screens. No matter what size, the screen acts like a mirror. Keep all bare-lamp sources and brightly lighted surfaces to the sides of the screen. Otherwise, visibility is lost. (See *For Television* in Chapter 7.)

Lighted louvered closet doors.

nontask surfaces

Accenting

Decorative wall-hung or freestanding items are not common in baths, but add to the ambience. Such decorative items can be accented with light. Adjustable recessed or surface-mounted fixtures can do the job with low- or line-voltage incandescent lamps. (See *Low Voltage* in Chapter 4 and *Ready-Made Recessed*

Decorative accents should be lighted.

Leaded-glass windows should be lighted from the outside.

Fixtures in Chapter 5.) However, if the art is precious, incandescent light fades colors. Use an ultraviolet filter to preserve irreplaceable art. (See *Accenting* in Chapter 7.)

Lighting enhances decorative interior finishes, such as deeply carved or louvered cabinet doors. Such cabinets should have grazing light to enhance the raised and lowered relief. (See *Wall Grazing* in Chapter 1 and *Underline Wall Texture with Grazing* in Chapter 5.) Glass-door cabinets can have low-voltage tube lights inside to illuminate the contents. (See *Inside Cabinet Lighting* in Chapter 7.) Faucets of highly polished metal and semiprecious stone can give back sparkle, if accented with light. Remember, only direct, incandescent light will create sparkle. Don't miss an opportunity to show off the finishes and fittings in baths.

Light leaded-glass windows at night from the outside to make them bright. Most of my clients are disappointed at night when their leaded-glass window does not look like it does in the daytime. If most of the glass is transparent, light must be reflected from leaves, fence, awning, or other outdoor feature to illuminate the window. The reflective surfaces should be pale in color, and increase the wattage to compensate for the loss from reflection and transmission. If most of the glass is translucent, direct light from floodlights can be used. However, angle the light from above or below the window to reduce the chance of glare. Illuminate leaded-glass whenever possible.

Architectural edges—tile overhangs at the countertop, toe spaces below lower cabinets, translucent dividers for toilets, steps, top of backsplashes, and under platforms of a raised hot tub or whirlpool—can be accented with low-voltage tubes. The tubes can be well hidden or surface mounted, depending upon the effect desired. (See *Low-Voltage Strips* in Chapter 5.)

Edges of divider walls with no doors can be accented with continuous, even light in the reveals. Often such walls are located between toilets and the rest of the bathroom. The reveal or sides of the opening can glow with light from floor back around to floor with a custom-made panel. The source can be cold cathode in any color and covered with a translucent opal lens, or can be a single MR source and prismatic material spreading the light evenly. Arch reveals are particularly emphasized with such light. (See *Arch Reveals or Recess Lighting* in Chapter 5 and *Cold Cathode* in Chapter 4.)

Architectural edges lighted by low voltage.

Edges of glass used in vanity tops, partitions, and divider walls can be edge lit. Use linear fluorescent or edge-lit fiber optics. The glass carries the light from a hidden source at the opposite edge of the glass to make the outside edge brilliant. Many baths use these marvelous glass features. Light them mysteriously and subtly with edge lighting.

Glass or plastic blocks are often foundations for tubs and whirlpools, are divider walls for toilets and showers, or are used as windows. Edge-lit fiber optics can light blocks with an MR source. The light can be one color with a filter or changing colors with a color wheel. Choose facetted blocks (ribbed, patterned, or distorted) to reflect as much light as possible. (See *Edge-Lit Fiber Optics* in Chapter 5.)

End-lit fiber optics offer delightful opportunities for creative decorative lighting in baths. The fibers inserted into countertops, backsplashes, walls, or ceilings create droplets of light in one color or change colors. (See *Decorative-Effect Fixtures* in Chapter 5.)

Low-voltage tubes can outline a glass di-

Arch recess lighting.

National Cathode

Prismatic film carries light.

LightPipe or 3M

vider between the toilet and the rest of the bathroom. Or tubes can create a glittering divider when curtain-hung. The effects are dramatic. Waterproof tubes can outline the ceiling of a shower stall, a bathroom skylight, or other architectural features.

A low-voltage panel of many, tiny low-voltage lights can be a divider. Likewise, a low-voltage panel can be a starlike or infinity pattern on the ceiling or wall with gold or blue-white light in a bronze or blue field. Such a panel would enlarge the space in a small bathroom. Creative designs are limitless with low voltage. (See *Decorative-Effect Fixtures* in Chapter 5.)

If a masonry wall is included in the bathroom, accent it with light. Graze the wall to get the greatest shadow patterns. (See *Underline Wall Texture with Grazing* in Chapter 5.)

Light for the Room Itself

Normally, bathrooms get enough light from task and nontask sources, but that is not always the case. If additional light is needed or task lighting cannot be installed where needed, consider using ready- or custom-made perimeter trough, cornice, or cove lighting. (See *Cornices, Coves, Low Voltage,* and *Recessed Perimeter Coffer* in Chapter 5.)

Heat for the room itself can come from an infrared R lamp in a ceiling recessed fixture. They are particularly useful for climates that have several months of neither heating or cooling. In such circumstances when a warm bathroom would be welcomed, the client need only heat the bathroom, not the whole house. A heat light would be more energy efficient and add general room illumination. (I have used them in many motels just to get enough light in the room for taking a bath.)

Light Outside the Room

Light the outside in one- and two-floor residences, where the bathroom has large uncovered windows. Otherwise, the windows turn black at night, and on the first floor the person inside might be concerned about what is outside. Typically, such bathrooms look out

Outline a divider.

Cove lighting for the room itself.

to an enclosed patio. Consequently, accent light can silhouette plant materials, graze textured surfaces, and/or create shadows. All extend the visual scene. Sometimes, the patio has a pool or pond which can reflect light from illuminated vertical elements (plants or architecture). Or the pool or pond itself can be illuminated to permit seeing through the water and creating a fourth dimension to the scene. Light outside balances interior light to prevent windows from reflecting glare from visible sources at night. Do not neglect the outside when lighting bathrooms.

Capri and Robert Long

dimming, protection, and energy

Programmable Dimmers

Baths are used for many activities, including relaxed bathing and/or vigorous body toning. Consequently, baths can have several different lighting moods. If the relaxing mode is a leafy, deep-toned bath and the exercising mode is TV news with enough light to read at the exercise machine, the multiple fixtures that supply these moods can be controlled by a programmable dimmer. Such dimmers permit three or four scenes and up to 2,000 watts per dimmer. The dimmer can be controlled remotely, bouncing the command off walls to the master dimmer box, which takes up only enough wall space for a three- or four-gang switch. Use them whenever possible. Even though four scenes might be judged to be excessive for a bath, in the long run, five or six will be wanted. Lighting is the best mood-motivation tool and programmable dimmers control light the best.

One major bathroom fixture manufacturer, who has used Warren Platner as a de-

signer, has a multifaceted dimmer that controls the total ambiance. The dimmer can control the lights, fill the tub with the chosen water temperature, turn on the stereo or TV, answer the phone, and even unlock the front door. The prepared ambiance can be accomplished by phone while on the way. Not bad!

Protective Electric Device

In baths, the National Electric Code requires that a ground fault interrupter (GFI) be on the electric circuit, if a wall receptacle is within 6 feet of water. The GFI can be either at the circuit-breaker panel or in a wall receptacle. The interrupters protect the electric appliance user from a fatal shock. (See *Protective Electric Devices* in Chapter 6.)

Protective Codes

Many state and local codes require watertight fixtures over tubs and showers. Rightfully so; water can cause hot glass to shatter. Even if not required, <u>never</u> use an open downlight over a tub or shower. Use a downlight with a watertight lens, identified as such in the manufacturer's catalog. Low-voltage tubes or panels can be made watertight at the factory. Fiber optics can be installed watertight and have a remote light source. Surface-mounted (wall sconces), hanging (chandeliers), and custom-made architectural fixtures (recessed coffer, luminous panels, etc.) for the most part are not watertight. Before determining the final lighting plan for a tub or shower check to make sure that any non-watertight fixtures are allowable.

Energy

States that are reducing energy use demand either energy-efficient lamps or fixtures. California, for instance, requires that at least one fixture in the room with the toilet be fluorescent (but not screw-based compact fluorescent) and requires that fluorescent be on the first wall switch. However, the efficiency requirement can be met in an adjacent room with plumbing. The intent is to save nonrenewable energy. Consequently, whether your state requires it or not, save energy. Specify the most energy-efficient lamps and fixtures and choose fluorescent whenever possible. If incandescent is required, use low voltage at low wattage. Energy efficiency could come from many low-wattage sources turned on only when needed, not a few high-wattage sources on all the time.

Baths can be effectively lighted with warm color fluorescent lamps, including the 30° or 35°K prime-color linear lamps and compact lamps. They render colors like incandescent and are energy efficient. Likewise, some low-voltage, direct-light fixtures can create sparkle. These bathroom fixtures can be positioned to provide good light on the surfaces without creating glare. In addition, many decorative effects are achievable with fiber optics, luminous ceilings, lighted skylights, and programmable dimmers. Bathroom light need not be lacklusterous.

chapter

9

what are your options for daylighting?

What are your options for daylighting in kitchens and baths? They are limited. The sources of daylight (sun and clouds reflecting sunlight) are constantly changing throughout the day. However, compass directions and altitude of the sun are predictable, but conditions of the sky are not. Hence, reliability is minimal. Apertures (windows, glass doors, and skylights) admit daylight and are determinable, but often cannot be specified by the person designing the lighting. The amount of light that enters can be too little or too much. Either way is not good.

too little sun or skylight

Too little sun or skylight makes a kitchen or bath dark and gloomy. Sometimes apertures are sufficient, but climate conditions are poor. Consequently, rooms do not get enough light. Sometimes apertures are too small or surface finishes are too dark. During daytime, not enough light is available to perform simple functions. Electric lights are turned on and often left on during the day. Electric lights were invented for use after dark. Why not augment the available light?

Daylight comes from the sun as energy in the form of light. It comes either directly from the sun or indirectly from the sky; it costs nothing. Using it as a source of free illumination is more important today than ever. Free illumination helps to conserve our precious nonrenewable resources.

See for Yourself #12: Do You Have Enough Daylight?

Can the sky be seen clearly through the window of a room exactly where reading, eating, or working will take place? If not, daylight will be insufficient for most tasks. If not, identify why.

Can the sky be seen clearly?

If not, probably not enough daylight will be available.

Often the causes of too little daylight can be corrected. If the causes are known, cures can be applied.

Cause: Weather Conditions

Clouds and smog can block the sunlight and diminish the reflected light from the sky. A clear view of the sky is essential in cloudy or smoggy conditions to gather as much daylight as possible. Therefore, if your client lives in these conditions, use the rule of thumb for enough daylight and add additional light with electric lighting.

Rule of Thumb for Enough Daylight

Have an unobstructed view of the sky from where any visual task is performed, seated or standing.

Cure: Cabinet or Furniture Arrangements

Poorly arranged cabinets and furniture can prevent sufficient daylight from reaching task surfaces. Rearrange any daytime work surfaces to take advantage of available light—but not glaring sunlight—from the window. Then daylight will be effective illumination.

COUNTERTOPS

Countertops and other work surfaces can be placed parallel or perpendicular to windows. However, they should not receive sun low in the sky at the time the work is likely to be performed (east for morning tasks and west for late afternoon). Also, never have the window behind the person working at the countertop, because a shadow would be cast on the work. If the countertop faces a brightly lit window, even if not in direct sun, additional electric light may be needed to balance the brilliance outside. The additional light is usually required in high-rise structures.

DESKS AND OTHER READING PLACES

Window light should come over the shoulder. Never face a window that could be very sunny, and never put a person's back to a window that is yielding very little light.

Cause: Are Windows Too Small or Nonexistent?

For minimal daylight in any room, the window area should be equal to 10 percent of the floor area. Therefore, a 10-by-10-foot room

Increase daylight with...

...more windows.

(100 square feet) needs 10 square feet of window. More will give more light, and under cloudy or smoggy conditions, the sun's heat will probably not be too much.

Cure: More Windows

For the best daylight, consider increasing the number of windows, rather than just increasing the size of one window. Position windows on different walls. The more walls with windows, the more daylight will be constant throughout the day. Likewise, glass in a door is considered a window and should be utilized whenever possible.

Cure: Skylights (For Owners)

Owners can use a skylight if they have access to the roof. Skylights are more than just holes in the ceiling. They are windows to the changing panorama of the sky—fast-moving clouds, treetops, changing sunlight, and, at night, a handful of stars and the moon. Skylights gather all the light possible. They are made of clear or nonclear glass or plastic. Some are equipped with interior screens, exterior awnings, built-in roller shades, or ventilation flaps. Some are domed; some are flat. Some are a single layer; some are double and sealed. They have increased in popularity twofold, according to a recent kitchen survey.

Tips for Skylights

- On sloped roofs, position skylights preferably on the north. Skylights gather so much light that north light is softer and better. Artists have known this fact for many years. If not possible on the north slope, then, in order of preference, east, south, and west are suitable. Skylights sloped to the south act as solar heaters, warming the space.
- On flat roofs with clear skylights, install a shade or other device to shut off the sun when it becomes too hot or too glaring.
- In a kitchen, a skylight toward the west will admit glaring afternoon sun, when the evening meal is being cooked. A skylight facing east or north would receive only reflected light in the afternoon. If a western orientation is the only choice, use nonclear glass or plastic to soften the light.
- In bathrooms, a skylight toward the east might thrust glare on the mirror in the morning. Make sure the sun's rays cannot reach the mirror. Bright but not glaring light is usually welcomed in the bathroom.
- Choose a nonclear skylight for rooms that contain carpeting, wallpaper, and fabrics that might fade, particularly if blue or purple.
- Choose a clear skylight for rooms that do not have delicately colored finish materials or artwork subject to fading, such as kitchens and baths.
- Use nonclear skylights when the view should be obscured; for instance, on flat roofs where leaves will pile up.

- Use nonclear skylights to soften too much direct sunlight.
- Choose a nonclear skylight where the ceiling brightness needs to be minimized.
- A clear skylight can be finished by boxing in the space between the ceiling and the roof. The boxed-in part will be as deep as the distance between the finished ceiling and the roof.
- For those who do not like a deep boxed-in effect, the ceiling should be finished with a flat nonclear plastic or glass diffuser.
- Even in cloudy or smoggy areas, some days are sunny. On these days, sunlight through clear skylights can cause blinding brightness and interfere with activities. Position the skylight so that the direct sunlight will fall where desired.

In spite of the cautions, clear skylights add a visual dimension to a room not possible with a window. The passing clouds and moon can be seen through them. On cloudless nights, moonlight is bright enough to allow people to move around without turning on any electric lights. In the winter, moonlit nights are brighter than early mornings.

(One of my client's sons reported to his mother in the morning that he could tell it was not time to get up for breakfast earlier, because the moon was too bright through the skylight in the bathroom. He said he know he had to wait until it was dark.)

Cure: Remove a Wall and Create a Sunroom

Owners of homes with an outside wall and condominiums with outside walls and balconies can remove the outside wall of the kitchen or bath and add a sunroom with a glass roof. The sunroom increases the potential for getting daylight, even if facing north. Sunrooms facing south catch as much daylight as possible from 10 am to 2 pm each day, summer or winter. The glass roof acts as a giant skylight. Be careful of the color and type of finish materials chosen for such sunrooms. Even in cloudy conditions, the brighter light will fade colors, some more than others—particularly the blues. And some finishes do not hold up with the additional heat from the daylight. Hard surface materials and neutral colors are best.

Cure: Glass Doors

Usually owners do not have access to the roof for a skylight. However, if owners have a solid

A clear skylight is usually recessed in the ceiling.

A diffuser on the ceiling eliminates the boxed-in look.

A glass door borrows light from another space.

door that faces a well-lighted space (interior or exterior), they can replace the solid door with a glass door. The glass door acts like a window, provided it is opposite brightly lighted windows in another room (preferably, windows facing south), a bright hallway with a skylight, or an outside door.

too much sunlight

Too much sunlight in kitchens and baths can have adverse effects. It is hot; it can be glaring. Sometimes it prevents people from sitting on one side of a kitchen table. Sometimes it prevents seeing well at a task surface. Likewise, sunlight can fade fabric, blister furniture, and bleach flooring.

Can the glare, heat, and harshness be shut out? Yes, the sun's light can be obscured or eluded. Obscure by blocking or scattering light with window treatments. Elude by getting away from direct light with cabinet or furniture arrangements, or by dark interior surfaces.

Where Is the Sun?

Where is the sun? The sun's location at various times of the day is predictable. In the early morning, the sun is low in the sky, rising to the highest elevation at noon standard time and descending at the end of the day. Simultaneously, the sun moves from an east-

erly direction in the morning to the south at noon, and to a westerly direction late in the day. The arc of that movement is larger in the summer than in the winter. In summer, the sun actually rises north-northeast and sets north-northwest; in winter it rises east-south-east and sets west-southwest. Consider this information in relationship to the windows.

What is the altitude of the sun? Knowing the angle above the horizon at various times of the day permits determining the position for a sun-control device. The sun is low to medium angles in the east and west, and highest in the south at noon each day. But the angle is different for each latitude. To determine the angle of the sun, know the latitude. In lower latitudes the sun is higher in the sky; in higher latitudes the sun is lower.

The sun is the highest in the summer, whatever the latitude, and lowest in the winter. All in all, remember that the sun is highest at noon in the summer at south windows and is low at east and west windows.

The sun can be controlled by sun-control devices—window treatments and/or external objects (trees, awnings, fences, etc.). Do not install any sun-control device before determining whether it would be effective. Develop this information by pretesting it with a pencil-and-paper or computer drawing.

Sun's arc.

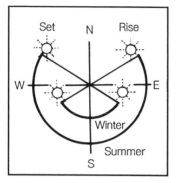

Angles of the sun.

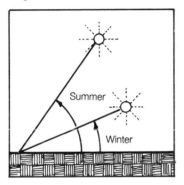

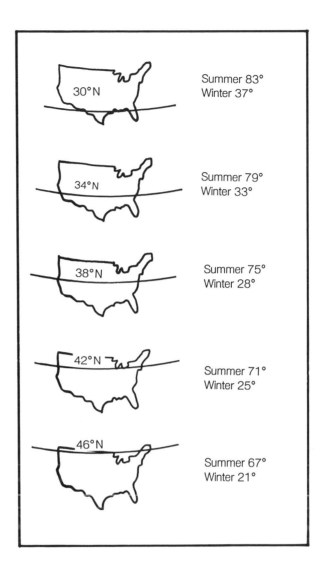

Sun's altitude at noon.

See for Yourself #13: Will a Sun-Control Device Work?

1. Determine the nearest latitude. (If halfway between two latitudes, divide the difference in half, adding the half to the lower number. Thus, if you live in Tampa, which is halfway between latitudes 26° and 30°, the summer angle would be 85° and the winter angle would be 39°.)
2. Make a small-scale drawing of the room and the surrounding walls, like a drawing of a doll's house cut in half, and a drawing of the device being tested, such as, an awning or a window shade.
3. Using a protractor, put the center point at the lower edge of the sun-control device—the bottom of the awning.
4. Project the angle of the sun at your latitude for both the summer and the winter directly into the room. Everything above the projected line from the sun would be in the shade; everything below the line would be in the sunlight.

This pretest will show the summer's sun penetration (the least) and the winter's sun penetration (the most). The effectiveness of a control device can be determined before installation to ensure that money is spent wisely.

What is the activity in the room? Sedentary activities are more likely to be disturbed by harsh sunlight than nonsedentary activities. For example, sitting at a kitchen desk and reading tax forms in harsh, hot sunlight would be more uncomfortable than making a store list by looking in the cabinets. Equally important, although many short-term activities are not affected by too much sun, some are. For example, brushing teeth is rarely affected, but putting on makeup is and requires sun control.

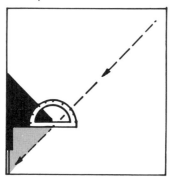

Use a protractor...

...to test a sun-control device.

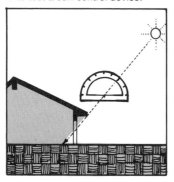

Window Locations

Windows and other apertures are the only ways that sunlight can enter a structure. Their location is important, and the direction they face determines when they receive sunlight.

Windows facing east receive direct light in the morning at a very low angle. Devices are necessary for kitchens with eating surfaces facing east.

Likewise, west windows receive sun directly in the afternoon in a decreasing angle until sunset. At that time of day it seems harsher and brighter. Therefore, sun-control devices are necessary for kitchen eating so that dinner and glaring light do not come together.

South windows receive sunlight between 10 a.m. and 2 p.m. In the summer, sun control is not usually needed. In the winter, sun control is sometimes needed, but since the sun warms, it is often welcome. Nonetheless, it is lower in the sky and penetrates deeper into the space. When heat is not wanted, daytime activities can be lighted by the sun, as long as sun controls are available.

North windows never receive direct sunlight. Light coming in a north window is reflected from somewhere else—the sky, the ground, or another building. North windows do not need any obscuring device.

How many and where windows are located are important. If only one wall has a window, the control device for that window governs sunlight for the whole space. If the device is heavy draperies and they are closed, direct sunlight is shut out along with all reflected skylight. Frequently, electric lights are turned on during the daytime to allow everyone to see, thereby consuming energy unnecessarily. If daylight is available, use it. In general, small rooms can manage with only one window, but larger rooms need additional walls with windows to get sun at different times of the day.

More daylight control is possible if two walls have windows. When one window receives direct light, it can be blocked and the other window can provide reflected light. More often than not, people seated in such a room are likely to face one window; and therefore, some form of sun control is necessary. Moreover, sometime during the day, at least one window will receive direct sunlight.

Similarly, windows on three walls and/or the roof (sun rooms) require sun-control devices. Kitchen eating and sink areas, and tubs often have window walls and skylights. Sometime during the day, two or three win-

Sun control for sunny windows.

Skylights gather the most light.

dows will receive sunlight. Therefore, any and all control devices are appropriate, particularly in kitchens. For greater control, use several devices.

Clerestory windows (windows high up on the wall) give good light, but direct sunlight can penetrate and fill the room with glare. Indoor controls are difficult to reach but not impossible if designed to be managed from the floor. Light can also be controlled with outdoor devices and ceiling color.

Skylights gather the greatest amount of sunlight possible, spreading it throughout the room. Like clerestory windows, skylight controls are difficult to reach. Therefore, consider using a skylight with a built-in louver or a motorized shade. If neither is available, drape a cloth, or use a large umbrella, wooden baffles, or landscape materials, inside or out, to soften the light. Baths and kitchens usually do not have delicate, fade-prone surfaces, and skylights might not require light control.

Methods of Control

WINDOW TREATMENTS

Block or scatter light with window treatments. A window treatment is putting something at

a window to reduce the sun's glare and harshness. However, it will not reduce heat unless insulated. A highly adjustable window treatment permits light from any angle to be redirected, scattered, and softened. They are best for sun control. Each type of window treatment has different degrees of adjustability and controls the sun at different angles.

Draperies

Draperies are the most common window treatments, but they are poor controls if windows are only on one wall. Depending upon the thickness of the material, draperies can either block or scatter the light. Dense material blocks; thin material scatters. When they are fully closed, dense draperies block the sun low in the sky. When they are partially closed, they sometimes block sun at oblique angles. Transparent drapes cannot block direct sun at all. If transparent drapes cover the window at all times, make sure that electric light is not also being used during the day. Daylight costs nothing and should be controlled in some other way.

Switchable Glass

Switchable glass can change from clear to frosted, thereby scattering the light (and also creating privacy). The change is produced by electrical current and liquid crystals, requiring about 1 watt per square foot of glass. Typically, it is used in commercial installation but has residential applications for baths and kitchens.

Grills, Screens, and Latticework

Grills, screens, and latticework scatter sunlight coming from an angle, but in most cases, they cannot be adjusted to control low sun. This treatment works best when the sun is high.

Shades

Shades can block all or part of a window. When part of the window is blocked, the rest transmits light from the sky or ground. To accomplish control, shades can be pulled from the top or the bottom. If pulled from the top, they block the sun high in the sky; if pulled from the bottom, they block low sun. Therefore, aesthetics or convenience alone should not determine which way to pull shades. Sun control should help.

Shutters

Shutters may be louvered or solid. Louvered shutters can adjust like venetian blinds and scatter light. Solid shutters block light completely or partially, depending upon their position.

Venetian Blinds

Venetian blinds are the most adaptable of the interior window treatments. They can deflect sunlight and redirect to illuminate the room. Light can be scattered up to the ceiling, down to the floor, or to the left and right, depending on whether the blinds are horizontal or vertical and how they are adjusted. Whatever the adjustment, blinds are the most versatile sun-control device. (Window manufacturers in Scandinavia make windows with the venetian blinds built between the layers, making them dust free.) Again, aesthetics alone should not dictate whether blinds should be vertical or horizontal. The decision should include control of light.

The color of a window treatment affects the color of light coming in through the window. Light picks up the tint of the color it strikes. Of course, it strikes the window treatment first. The best color for a window treatment is neutral or near neutral; the worst is an intense color that distracts or becomes a source of glare itself. Choose a color that gives no unwanted effect of its own to the interior space.

Window construction is important because it creates sun control. Ideally, sun control should be accomplished by structural gradations from brightness of the outside to dimness of the inside. Windows in older homes created such a gradation. They were embedded in thick walls. They had deep sills, tapered wood between glass panes, and movable shutters both inside and out. On the contrary, windows in contemporary buildings are placed in thin walls, offering little to soften the light, especially in curtain-wall high rises. Recessed windows create a gradual gradation of light from the sky to the room. Bay and bow windows function as recessed windows if depth of the bay or bow is great enough to shade the interior space from direct sunlight. Special attention must be paid to deliberately soften light at and around windows.

Awnings

Awnings on the outside can block light. They can be either adjustable or nonadjustable. They can have side panels, blocking the sun from high, medium, and low oblique angles. Awning material has shorter life expectancy than the structure to which it is attached. But they are decorative and add to the ambience, besides being functional.

Sunshielding Glass

Patterned and sunshielding glass or plastic cut down sunlight in different amounts. Patterned glass diffuses light unless the sun is aiming directly at it. Then, light appears brighter than through clear glass, because the pattern augments and makes light brilliant in the way that cut glass does. (Patterned glass is most often used in shower stalls.) Sunshielding glass or plastic is either reflective or tinted. Reflective glass or plastic bounces back between 8 and 80 percent of the sun's light, depending upon its manufactured characteristics. Tinted glass or plastic bounces back 6 to 8 percent. However, direct sunlight is a problem for these sunshields, too. Question the supplier carefully to determine the exact amount and type of sun control. In high rises, where other architectural options for sun control are limited, sunshielding glass or plastic is a must; in low-rise structures it can be useful.

CABINET AND FURNITURE ARRANGEMENTS

Sun can be eluded by getting away from its light. One method is to arrange the cabinets and furniture away from sunlight. Arrangements to avoid sunlight are not employed often. They should be, particularly with south windows. With any arrangement or window exposure, several rules of thumb should be followed to elude sunlight.

Rules of Thumb for Cabinet and Furniture Arrangements

Work surfaces, tabletops, and desks should not be next to windows that receive direct sunlight at the time of day when the surfaces would be used.

Sofas, chairs, and lounges should not face bright, glaring windows, particularly if the seat is bathed in the sun.

Sunny window walls
should not be dark in color.

In a low-rise structure, furniture arrangements for eating should not require a seat to face an unprotected east window (at breakfast time) or unprotected west window (at dinnertime). In a high rise, the sun would probably be below the level of the west window at dinner time.

INTERIOR FINISHES

The second eluding method is to cover major surfaces away from apertures with colors that absorb some of the bright light. Reduce daylight at the surface it falls on. Dark interior finishes can effectively absorb light, but do not use them adjacent to an aperture. The dark surface and the bright direct sunlight will be glaring. Dark ceilings, back walls, floors, and/or cabinets can absorb sunlight. Use them!

All major interior surfaces—floors, walls, and ceilings—are finished in a color. Sunlight striking these surfaces will be absorbed and reflected back in the quantity allowable by the color of that surface. Dark colors (dark blue, black, deep brown) reflect only a small percentage of light. Pale colors (beige, white, pale yellow) reflect most of the light received.

The floor receives most of the direct sun-

light in any room. A dark floor (wood stain, carpet or other dark floor covering) can reduce the amount of light by absorption.

The wall containing the window is the most critical wall for eye comfort. If the window receives direct, unrelenting sunshine, the window wall should not be dark. It should be pale so that no harsh contrasts are created.

Contrary to the usual practice, white walls should not be used where windows receive unrelenting sunlight. In sunny climates and in high rise structures, windows are more likely to receive direct sunlight for long periods of time. Consequently, white walls are too bright, creating an unpleasant brightness that does not subdue the outside brightness. Instead, use a pastel or a color that reflects only 70 percent of the light. Many shades and colors are available in this reflectance range. How much does a color reflect? Ask the local paint store for technical paint samples. These samples list light reflectance values, indicated by "LR%." The percentage refers to the amount of light reflected; the amount remaining is light absorbed.

Walls adjacent to the window receive sunlight. If walls are dark, they become harsh contrasts. Finish them with a high light-reflecting color, but not necessarily white.

The back wall can be finished in a dark color. It does not contrast with bright sunshine and helps to absorb excess light.

Ceilings also can be dark to absorb light, since direct sunlight reaches the ceiling only very early or very late in the day. Dark ceilings help control light from clerestory windows if no other control device is possible.

CABINET AND FURNITURE COLORS

Any cabinet and furniture, particularly a desktop or other work surface that receives direct sunlight, should be finished in a nonglossy, pale color to avoid eye-fatiguing contrast. But cabinets and furniture away from direct sunlight can be dark, thereby absorbing some light. (Mediterranean countries use dark furniture; for example, Greek Cottage and Country Italian furniture.)

Interior cabinet and furniture colors will appear truer in bright daylight, but appear washed out in intensely bright sunlight. Cabinet and furniture colors will appear duller and darker in dim daylight. Consequently, if a kitchen has northern window exposure and will be used during the day, dark cabinets might not be the best choice, if daylight is to be the primary daytime source. In the same manner, bathrooms used during the day in an active daytime residence should not have dark cabinets unless the bath has a southern window exposure or a skylight.

Even though options for daylight con-trol are limited when compared to the many options for electric light, the options are powerful and most people are awake longer during daylight hours than dark hours. Consequently, design with daylighting for the most effective lighting scheme.

daylight, electric light, and tasks

If the kitchen desk uses daylight as a light source, remember that lighting principles hold true for both electric light and daylight. Glare positions do not care whether the source is a lamp or the sun. Never have a person sitting at a desk facing a bright sunny window. It creates direct and reflected glare. Never have a computer on a kitchen desk face a sunny window. It creates glare on the screen. The window should be on the left for right-handed people and on the right for left-handed people —opposite the hand used for writing. If light at the window is too bright, equalize it with brighter electric light on the desk from nonglare positions. If light at the window is too dull, illuminate the desktop and the room with enough electric light to balance the daylight. When light at the window fades after sunset, replace it with electric light from the same side of the room, thereby preserving the same balance of lighting. (Well-designed light from any source is well designed.)

If a kitchen or bath has only one window and that window is in view when the

Balance bright direct daylight with electric light.

A task may need localized light even with a window.

St. Charles

St. Charles

140   Chapter Nine

person is doing a task (e.g., at the sink or the mirror), the direct sunlight or the daylight might be too bright. Never have a bright uncovered window in view when a long-term task takes place. If a short-term task takes place, additional electric light within the space could balance the bright window for the duration of the task. Use general or task illumination to create the balance.

If a kitchen or bath has more than one window, room balance is easier to obtain with daylight. Use the various methods of window control in this chapter, but a task might need localized lighting to be sufficiently illuminated. Use portable fixtures for short-term tasks or built-in fixtures for long-term tasks.

All in all, designers have many options for utilizing daylight and specifying the best possible electric light. The power of light is undeniable. The technology of lighting is full of choices. The art of lighting is resplendent with aesthetic decisions. Design lighting thoroughly and effectively. Awaken color with light. Bring out highlight. Put down a shadow. Capture attention. Create a mood. Determine what is desirable to be seen in a kitchen or a bath. Put a visible source where it enhances as jewelry. Build-in lighting for hidden sources. Control daylight as though it were an installed source. Do not miss out on any of the options. Everyone recognizes good lighting; both the space and the user benefit from it.

index